# THE TREE OF KNOWLEDGE IS MARY'S SWEET VINE

## BELLA LOUISE ALLEN

authorHOUSE®

AuthorHouse™
1663 Liberty Drive
Bloomington, IN 47403
www.authorhouse.com
Phone: 1 (800) 839-8640

Published by AuthorHouse  04/25/2018

ISBN: 978-1-5462-3956-7 (sc)
ISBN: 978-1-5462-3957-4 (hc)
ISBN: 978-1-5462-3955-0 (e)

Library of Congress Control Number: 2018905066

Print information available on the last page.

Any people depicted in stock imagery provided by Getty Images are models,
and such images are being used for illustrative purposes only.
Certain stock imagery © Getty Images.

This book is printed on acid-free paper.

KJV
Scripture taken from The Holy Bible, King James Version. Public Domain

NIV
Holy Bible, New International Version®, NIV® Copyright ©1973, 1978, 1984,
2011 by Biblica, Inc.® Used by permission. All rights reserved worldwide.

NLT
Holy Bible, New Living Translation, copyright © 1996, 2004, 2015
by Tyndale House Foundation. Used by permission of Tyndale House
Publishers, Inc., Carol Stream, Illinois 60188. All rights reserved.

ESV
The Holy Bible, English Standard Version. ESV® Text Edition: 2016. Copyright
© 2001 by Crossway Bibles, a publishing ministry of Good News Publishers.

Bella Louise Allen

# THE TREE OF KNOWLEDGE IS
# MARY'S SWEET VINE

*A love story that began before the beginning of time*
*For the future generations of God's children*

Photo By: Shutterstock

## Bella Louise Allen

# *Acknowledgements*

First and foremost, for my friend, confidante, and publishing consultant at Author House Publishing. I want to thank Scott Hensley for listening to my needs as a first-time author and guiding me through the process of publishing my first two books: *Miracles among Chaos* and *Love Letters in the Sand.*

I cannot fully express my gratitude for the endless hours of personal time Scott has taken to read, edit, and listen to my story. He is an exceptional man and professional leader in the publishing industry.

My gratitude goes out to my friend and editor Tina Passman. I want to thank Tina for the love and advice she has given me as I walk through the learning process of the awakening. Without Tina's additional support and advice, it would have been a much harder path to follow.

Heartfelt thanks, goes out to my sister Helen Golding. Without Helen's support throughout the years and her own knowledge of the awakening process, I wouldn't have been able to stay as grounded as I have. Learning to let go of the past and moving past fear has been one of the greatest lessons I have learned from her. I only hope that through the books that I have written I can give back to you, in some way, the love you have given to me. I hope to honor your own journey through these amazing books of love, light, faith and hope. Your own journey walking beside me has helped me overcome my fears and has led me straight into the loving arms of Jesus Christ.

**Dedicated with love to my children**
To: Sherri Linn, David Nathan, II and Paul Allen, Sr., the center of my world and the reason I write books of love, light, faith and hope for the future of all our children.


**And to my grandchildren**
Curtis Lovell, Ayla Faith, David Nathan, III, Skye April and Paul Jr.: You are the sunshine in my life and the reason I continue to love and send light out to others. You are special angels sent to help me learn. You are my very special heroes. You are each special and unique in your own way.

# Contents

# Introduction

What does it mean to give one's life fully to God? What does it mean to truly take up your cross and follow Jesus Christ? What does it mean to be strictly obedient to the will of God, no matter where it leads?

History has shown the challenges, difficulties, sorrows, and joys of many faithful women we remember and praise and learn from today. St. Catherine of Siena, St. Catherine of Genoa, St. Mary of Agreda, St. Gertrude, St. Margaret Mary, St. Faustina – these are only a few names of Our Lord's Prophet-Brides, consecrated women to whom He spoke, with whom He walked, and from whom He required obedience, devotion, and the recording of His Words.[1]

Not all were cloistered, very few were from a privileged class or well-educated. Some had assistance in the almost unimaginable obligation and task of recording the experience of this intimate relationship with God. Some worked alone. Few were acknowledged in their lifetimes. Many were called mad.

In His handmaids, Our Lord chose those who were humble of heart, the pure of soul, those with the simplicity of unwavering devotion. Although dedicated to Jesus, each soul was sought out and asked to fulfill a task by Our Lord. The freedom of individual agency was always emphasized; when once the blessed soul gave her "yes," a period of intense and difficult work ensued. In some cases, the health of the chosen one was affected, and the task was carried on through dictation or great effort in writing. In several cases, death came shortly after.

Within the limitations of the language, culture, and education of each faith-filled and faithful woman, they strove to complete their tasks.

---

[1] See bibliography

Their tasks, in one way or another, instructed and renewed the Church. We can read their works today. They use the language of the body, of sensuality, as well as the language of the soul, of spirituality. At some point, these languages merge, in a place past earthly meaning, for union with God is indescribable in its ecstasy.

The individual whom Bella Louise Allen calls St. Julie Ann is one such soul. What you are about to read is the story of her extraordinary love affair with God/Jesus Christ. It is the story of what total abandonment to Christ while living in the world is like. For Jesus Christ came to her, breathed life into her, and loved (and loves) her. She, in turn, loved (and loves) Him. At times, the point of view or the statements may be difficult, but the message that Jesus, through St. Julie Ann, is sending, rings clear. It is the message of all the Prophets: *God is love. God loves all His children. God suffers at the evil deeds of His children. God is seeking you, and your love. Repent. Change your hearts. Come home. For the End is truly at hand!*

Mary, the Blessed Mother of God, plays an essential role here. She is to gather Her children to her, sheltering us beneath her cloak. Delegated by Our Lord, she continues her role as our fierce and protective Mother, fighting for us through time and space, Blessed Mother of Our Lord, Blessed Lady. She comes to us in Mexico to Leponto, at Fatima and Lourdes, in the battlegrounds and slums and famine-ravaged world of today. The Alliance of Hearts, beating as One, forms a major theme of this work.

It has been my privilege to come to know Bella Louise Allen, and to closely read and slightly edit her words. It is my hope that the Church she loves will come to accept the Messages she records.

Kristina Maria Therese Nielson

Easter 2018 ad majorem Dei gloriam

# Preface

## CHRIST HAS RISEN...

3:44 a.m.
December 25, 2017

The miracle was so long ago. The dear Savior's birth, celebrated today by Christians and non-Christians alike, keeps God's love alive through this great event. Keeping God's promise through the ages.

The greatest gift given on this night was not the gifts of myrrh, frankincense or gold, but the birth of our dear Lord, in the form of a homeless babe, through the power of God. Mother Mary carried this miracle within her own womb. A blessed young woman of faith and love, Mary's life was defined that night. At 16 years of age, she gave birth to the Savior of the world. It was a great honor for her and would be a great sorrow.

Little did Mary know the fate of her precious Babe. God knew His Son's fate would end in torture and torment for Him and for the Mother of God and all those who had come to love Jesus Christ.

Today, as then, the world is in turmoil and His Mission comes to life once more. A faithful woman of God holds tight to Jesus Christ's hand and He leads her back in time and reminds her of history and the true reason for the season of Christmas: family, life, and love were the reasons for the Lord's birth, along with fulfillment of prophecy and bringing salvation to a nation in ruins.[2]

---

[2] Jesus came first to fulfill the prophecies of His coming to the children of Israel, oppressed under Roman occupation. Later, His Mission expanded to the Gentiles. Bib refs.

**God shares with me that time is an illusion** His children are in need of a resurrection story of their own. They must gaze in wonder again as out of the tomb Salvation and love return. This new story comes through another faithful child of God. Saint Julie Ann, writing as the Handmaid of the Lord, tells of a new journey handed to her after her own lost soul was found worthy of a second chance by God Himself.

This book of love, light, faith, and hope - containing God's own truth's – has come into being for all those willing to read, understand, and comprehend the deep messages of love that have been recorded by God's own Divine Mercy Angel.

Saint Julie Ann's destiny has always been to shine love and light. God shares with her the patterns and genealogy from the Bible and their importance to souls today. God has always taught life after death and resurrection. Today, His love and power can be seen again in this new book that has been written by the hands of God's own chosen bride.

Christ is risen. Mother Mary has taken over the bodily vessel of this sweet angel of mercy, Saint Julie Ann. Through her, the Blessed Mother is proving God's love and power to the children of the world. The Messages continue. The Mother of God, the Father and Creator of the world write their Lessons of love and mercy through the eyes of Saint Julie Ann. May all who read this book find the deep passionate love that God has for each and every one of you. Peace on earth and good will to all of God's children throughout eternity.

Bella Louise Allen

Photo: By Shutterstock

*Matthew 28:6 (KJV) He is not here; for He is risen, as he said. Come, see the place where the Lord lay.*

# Prologue

10:00 a.m.
September 17, 2017

## The Tree of Life

God proves His immense power this morning. He shows me repeatedly His love above all that He brings forward.

This is the resurrection of love from the beginning of time. God tells me. ***"You are my own. You are my light and my love."*** [3]

God and I connect this morning and we just hold one another. I lay on my bed on my stomach and I hear God's heart beat beneath my head. I hear God's heart beat within my ear. I feel God's heartbeat within my own chest.

This understanding and love that God and I hold for one another is so very powerful. As we love this morning like a real husband and wife I feel His arms surround me. I feel God's arms touch my skin. I cry tears this morning, for I wish I could see Him.

I walk and talk daily with the Creator of the world. He tells me I have captured His heart and He shows me His love many times and we connect as one.

God tells me many things as we converse. We write, however, about the Tree of Life.

---

[3] All words of God are in bold Italic print and quotation marks.

God takes me on a journey back before the beginning of time. We go to the Tree of Life and I see the tiny leaves on this tree. I have heard of this tree and I have seen it depicted in art. Drawn to it, I even have a necklace of the Tree of Life.

I see the green leaves first on the Tree of Life and then I see one single berry. This berry is transparent. As Jesus stands beside me, I see the red within this berry and God indicates that this represents His blood. The clear fluid that I see within this berry represents plasma. Plasma, as I understand it, is the healing after the bloodshed is released from the body.

Jesus sits with me beneath this tree and as we sit I feel Jesus turn into God. God and I sit under the Tree of Life and He calls me Mary. God asks me to take on the role, the name, and the identity of the Mother of God.

God and I sit under the Tree of Life this morning and I see Jesus and myself. We are naked. Life is at its best and God and I are completely in love. We both feel this powerful love. The ecstasy that I feel within my body is the kisses of the "*Life Force of God*". My body is made up of angels and saints.

God holds me tight under the Tree of Life. He tells me as he brushes my hair to the side of my neck how much He has always loved me, through all the lives I have lived. My soul-purpose becomes clear this morning and God's heart is light and full of joy.

He retells the history of Adam and Eve. He reminds me how the first disobedience led to Jesus Christ on the cross at Calvary. He reminds me of those who followed Him: Saint Margaret Mary, Saint Bernadette and Saint Faustina. He then takes me to my own birth.

God tells me I have always been a special child. I have always held love in my heart for everyone that I meet. My smile has always captivated

Him. He wrote my story. God has written all the stories throughout history. [4]

We all have a purpose and a plan, and mine, God tells me, is a great one.

## My Mission

As I lie in bed with my Lord God and Creator, I ask Him to just love me. Tears flow to the sheets beneath my face and I feel the kisses of the angels who make up who I am. I feel the Life Force of God more strongly every day. My heart vibrates, and I feel my scalp tingling. I feel arousal throughout my body and God proves His love for me and that He is ever present within me this morning. Our consciousness is one. We have fully merged.

God brings Mother Mary's face to my vision this morning and I see her, and she is lovely and beautiful. She is lightly veiled, and He asks me to take the covering from her face.

*"Continue to walk with Me and love with Me, Mary."*

*"Our children are so lost, and they need the love of your pure heart."*

*"Your fun- loving ways can show them all the love I hold for each of them."*

*"Their fears keep holding them back from knowing who they truly are."*

*"Teach them the lessons I have taught to you."*

God reminds me of the story of Lazarus.[5] He says it is never too late to bring a soul back into the Light of God. It is always possible to bring life back, even from the dead. [6] God wants the souls and hearts of His children to turn toward His love and light. God has much faith in my abilities to love and shine a light brightly on these mysteries of life and

---

[4] Jeremiah plans
[5] John 11:43
[6] bib. Everything is possible with God.

death. It starts with the mysteries behind the devil, who is given so much power in the thoughts of human beings.

I have conquered and faced so many demons in this life. God tells me, **"There is no stronger woman who could make such a change or movement of love happen as quickly as you."**

## HIS CAPTIVE HEART

*Lost and all alone*
*The night grows deathly quiet*
*Deep purple and blackened skies loom over the world*
*Tears of anguish flood my eyes*
*The blood drips red and deep from my heart tonight*
*His captive heart is lonely and sad*
*Not sure where to turn*
*Where to go from here*
*Children crying, dying in the light of day*
*Sobbing in the night*
*Their cries can be heard*
*They are unaware of their worthiness*
*Of God's love*
*His captive heart is tortured and bleeding*
*Still today*
*Hung from the cross and yet no one see's it but*
*Mother Mary; she is God's truest love and light*
*God's own captive heart locked up within*
*The walls of a pure saint's heart*
*Many tearful nights have led her to this realization*
*The Holy Spirit lives within each of us*
*Lost souls too many and Jesus Christ's Sacred Heart fades*

God has brought forward this idea before. As I walk and talk daily with the Creator of the world I have come to understand that His heart fades daily as our children run from His love and light.

The destructive energies and entities that surround and overwhelm our children are affecting God's Sacred Heart.

I am the Mother of God. I have divine knowledge and understanding. I have accepted and do accept God's proposal for marriage. I say, "Let it be done unto me according to thy word." I willingly accept the enormous responsibility of bringing love, light, faith, and hope to the children of the world. I can begin through my own love story. My love story is the greatest love story of all. My story is the never-ending love of God and Mother Mary for our children.

*

My emotions flow freely today, and the tears come and go. I understand all that God has given to me and I fear only the time that stands in our way.

I am a woman who knows how to make things happen and I give it up to God. His own divine timing is what must happen.

God asks if He can write a poem. I struggle to let His love flow to the pages and He knows it.

## THE MOTHER OF GOD

***When I let go of what I am, I become what I might be. Lao Tzu***
*Who is this woman who stands before me?*
*Her hair golden*

*Her tears sparkle*
*I, the Father, wipe away these sweet tears*
*No love can compare to this love*
*The Mother of God*
*My masterpiece*
*Purest heart*
*My soulful Saint*
*Her smile fades and then returns*
*Pierced heart pierced*
*Severe teachings*
*Who is this woman who stands before me?*
*Child's heart*
*Gold heart*
*Heart twin to my own*
*Loving heart*
*Deep*
*True*
*Keeper of My heart*
*She keeps It beating strong*
*The Mother of God*
*Her tears My tears*
*Blood tinged*
*Flowing*
*Over*
*Her*
*The torment is Mine*
*From Heaven*
*I ask*
*"Marry Me, My love"*
*"We will bring about New Heaven, New Earth"*
*Who is this woman?*
*The Mother of God*
*Mystery*
*Majesty*
*You*

\*

As we shower this morning, we love through the heart, and I feel the deep connection as the water comes down on our body. My thoughts are His and the love we feel turns into tears as I remember a special angel, a woman I only met once or twice. Her passing was a terrible loss for the family of my Godmothers.

Lisa was a woman who loved hard and taught others of God's love and light while she was here. In an accident early one morning, less than a mile from her own house, God called her home to heaven. She left a loving husband and five precious babies behind.

I see Lisa's babies. They are lost lambs without their mother. So much pain!

Memories of my own come rushing in. A flood of grief washes over me, and I feel the arrows pierce my heart. Lisa and her whole family suffered tragedy and carried heavy crosses.

This is just one small glimpse for me of the hard journey that God shares with me. In this connection with God I see things that are horrific through the eyes of God and the angels and Saints I carry within.

I try to wash these visions from my eyes. My memories join the memories of the aching that God reveals from Lisa's sweet babies. Arrows pierced their hearts at such a young age!

*

**Lessons for each of us; some ills we bring on ourselves**

A Teaching from God this morning as I shower: *"We can all make this world better."*

The three-way plan is on the way to destruction. God sees it and I know it in my heart.

*Lesson: The three-way plan:*

*God's Way: To live righteously. "I am the way and the truth, and the life. To love and Be-Loved.*

*Your way: To run from God's love and light. To run in fear. To judge others. To want things of material value, not wanting love or being love.*

*The Highway-to-hell: To live for things 'of' this world. To live with greed, lust, anger, and hate in your heart. Not caring for your brethren and running with the 'devil'.*

We can make a difference with the mission and quest for Salvation that God has shown me. Through writing down His words, I hold the key to unlock God's own truths for the children of the future, teaching and giving love and light.

God has set the table for the Last Supper and I am the host with the knowledge that needs to be shared. I hold tight to Jesus' arm and wait for His plans and dreams to come true.

# Part I. HIS HOLY GRAIL:
## The Missing Links

Photo By: Shutterstock

*Share this cup of blessing In His name, remembering how He; Himself took the cup in the upper room, as the hour of His crucifixion drew near and said, "this is My blood which is shed for many—do this in remembrance of Me.*

## Captive of His Heart

*The missing Sanskrit Tablets, written and lost.[7] Scrolls destroyed.* I am still given puzzle pieces and I know not what the end results will be.

---

[7] St. Thomas brought the Good News to India. There is also a strong tradition in India that Jesus spent time there. This tradition regarding Jesus is best known in Pakistan. St. Thomas, arriving ca. 50 C. E., established Christianity in Kerela and along the south east coast. In my visions, these tablets in Sanskrit from India contained important information about Jesus and Mary.

Mysteries revealed, and empty pieces hollow my heart, unfolding one breath at a time. I feel lost and alone.

Prophecy is revealed to a lonely child of God. She tries to save the world from a chair. Chained to His heart, she is unable to breathe on her own. She receives Messages from the other side from a lost soul. God feels pain and sorrow for a world quickly drowning in a sea of His own Blood shed.

She was consciously unaware of this eminent fate over eleven years ago when she was locked up in a prison of her own, searching and reaching out from a body that turns out to be that of someone else. Plans were revealed to her and she had no idea where to turn but to Jesus Christ.

Jesus tried to teach her many great mysteries and her own reality was taken from her three times. He came back time after time and knew of her ability to get this special project to where it needs to be.

She received Messages of, *'seals broken and hearts bleeding'*. Tears of blue flowed from her eyes as Jesus wept through her body. It was a painful Awakening. He told her, ***"I am sorry."*** He shared - and shares - a love with her which had been written since before the beginning of time.

She struggled daily to follow God's breath. She heard Him within her heart. She failed and fell. Each time, He picked her up. (He considers perseverance a great virtue.) She worked tirelessly to find the values that were not given to her as she grew up; there were many lost souls in her family.[8]

After writing two books as "training exercises," she learned to hear Him, she learned to process His Messages and Visions, she said "yes" to Him in every way. And, so it began.

\*

---

[8] As told in *Miracles among Chaos*, by the author.

God asks me to write this book I have no idea where it will lead me. I love Him. My heart belongs to Jesus Christ. I ask Him questions, and I only fear failing Him.

Messages from the other side? No, from within my heart. His heart is mine and I wake up to it beating as if it lies on my body. Such an exhilarating feeling and a love felt like no other!

Awareness, meditation and prayer are of utmost importance for my journey with God to be successful. Connecting to my center, my heart. It is pure and white, and it roars words, phrases, and songs.

I wonder what these next pages will reveal? I hold my breath and pray for His love to shine through the words Jesus helps me put to paper. I feel a sense of urgency. For my world, His world, and your world depend on His messages through me.

The world is upside down and Jesus has come to me in His flesh form to rectify all the bad choices made. Who, what, when, where and how is this to be done? Answers only God knows: *"I am that I am"*. I am a vessel of His love and a faithful servant of the Lord.

*Lesson: We humans pay a price for our choices. Jesus tried to teach us during His ministry on earth, and He tries to teach us now. How often do we forget to read His words in Scripture! How often do we fail to sit and listen to our inner selves! What we call our higher consciousness is that voice of God we hear and question or obey daily. Failing or succeeding in all we do is solely in our hands, based on the choices He places before us.*

God reveals to me that His heart is fading from the inside out. It fades one breath at a time. He shows me how His breath is taken away as each day passes and I feel it, breathless and painful, within my own lungs. I am not sure how much I can take. He tells me, ***"You are your mother's daughter."***

3

God gave me my wings of gold in a dream.[9] An amazing gift! He allows me to feel them. They grow and become stronger every day. I only wonder if they will carry me away before I am able to reach the people to whom He is trying to get His special messages. Before it is too late.

# THE HOLY TRINITY

*"A blessed day, and I love you more today than yesterday,*
*but not nearly as much today as I will tomorrow!"*
After many months of tearful messages, my world is turned upside down yet again today. I attended Mass at St. John's Catholic Church. It was truly marvelous. I experience a feeling of love like no other as God walks with me every step of the day. A life filled with His Holy Spirit.

I arrived a few minutes early to enjoy the beauty within the walls of this magnificent church. My failed marriage of twenty-three years was blessed here. My three children were baptized at St. John's. My sweet friend's daughter's death was celebrated here, and now I enter the doors, a new woman, and a saved child of God.

I have always been a wanderer, and God reminds me of so many memories on this journey. He reveals to me blueprints of my own journey. Lives from before the beginning of time. He reminds me to hold my identity from this lifetime close to me; it has kept me strong for the journey that He says is to help Him bring so many of His lost lamb's home.

I pray for strength and guidance on this early morning, on this beautiful day. I struggle to fight tears. As strong as God says I am, I am still just a woman kneeling before Him asking for His love to shine through the vessel of my body for all His children.

The music is beautiful. Each part of God's love is present in the whole ceremony this morning. God asks me to notice His greatness through

---

[9] Wings of gold symbolize sainthood.

the Catholic Church. I see His very faithful children, those that sit amongst Him and me this morning. Our family.

I am reminded of many meditations over the past twenty-three months. (God asks me to remember all that He has taught me.)

After receiving communion, He gives me this sensory manifestation:

*I feel sick to my stomach and the pain is unbearable. A wave of nausea engulfs my entire body. I kneel and pray for forgiveness of my own sins and that of all of God's lost lambs. God shares with me that the consecrated bread is His flesh. I feel the host as flesh in my mouth. He shares with me the taste of blood in my mouth. The consecrated wine is His blood. His blood runs through my veins.*

*Tears well up behind my eyes. His hands are covered in blood. His children are killing one another too fast. His children are dying needlessly, dying out of fear and ignorance. God then shares the vision of His flesh as raw and close to the surface of His bones.*

Jesus holds my hands as I try not to cry out.

I try with all my might to process this message from Mass, so I can continue with my day. God shares with me this journey I am on with Him will not end. [10]

He is so glad that I am all that I am.

After Mass I visit with my friend and confidant. I share only what God guides me to share with those who He sees will benefit me on my journey.

The experience today has been difficult. God knows my own heart is heavy.

---

[10] I want God to know I can be who He wants me to be. I never want Him to leave me!

Later in the evening as I walk hand and hand with Jesus, I reflect on the day's events. He brings me more love than I thought could exist.

The sky is pink and lavender tonight and the sun is just creeping down over the tree lines. I am mesmerized by all His Creation tonight.

An emotional day, yet God brings me clarity on who I am and the reason behind His choice of me for this journey. The histories He has shown me are true and real. I have been with God since before the beginning of time. I am His feminine side. His Eve in the Garden of Eden. I am His Most Immaculate Heart, Mother Mary. I was His most precious Son, hung from the cross. I am God's most precious bride today. I am His prophet to help bring His love and light to the children of the world. My mission is to help secure a future for our children.

God tells me, ***"You are the Holy Grail of today."***

God has revealed to me great mysteries and I can't find enough time to record them all. I am but one woman struggling to stay present in each moment. God holds my hand and walks me back in time and then shows me the dim future. I stay humble and am filled with grace as God shares more with me. My Immaculate Heart is fully connected to Jesus' Sacred Heart. We have merged fully - mind, body and spirit.

Drawings of love and messages coincide with all of God's love letters to me. Poetry for all to see His deep love for me and the love I hold for Jesus Christ.

Dreams are coming nightly, and I can't share them all.

In meditation, I receive the deepest insight to our journey as a husband and wife as we fully connect within the silence of my heart.

I move forward with our writing and wait patiently for word from the Catholic Church.

## THE TRINITY REVEALED:

*"In June of 2014 I was awakened to all of God's love". "The Holy Spirit took over my entire body".*

God's precious vision and prophecy again is here. His only begotten Son has returned.

As He wakes me with the gentle rain on the first day of autumn, with the new season comes the necessity of change. Change must be accepted, and love must grow.

His children are in danger of extinction.

God shares with me a new vision and it is the most painful sight He could share with me. He shows me Jesus on the cross. His feet are nailed to the cross and His hands are bound and nails pierce through to the wood from which He hangs. *From which I hang ...*

*Stabbing pain everywhere. The weight of my body crushing my lungs. Blood runs down my face from my gouged head and drips past my eyes swollen shut. I can barely see through the slits. I taste my blood. **"Do this in Remembrance of Me."** I see her, my mother. Blessed Mary sobs out her Son's agony and tears fall from our eyes. A spear has pierced my side. The sharp tearing blow rips my final breath from my agonized chest. **"It is finished."***

I am reminded of my thirst. I am reminded of my journey. I am reminded of His need for our love. Too much pain and so many tears shed. He shows me He is not known to His children who need Him most.

A most sorrowful vision, and His lost lamb and sacrifice today is me. Through drawings, dreams and meditation God through Jesus Christ brings all my truths forward.

*Interlude*: I walk, talk, dance, sing and write love letters daily to the children of the world.

Jesus prepared me over the past eleven years for this day. I walked the halls of our local mental facility and I saw His prophecy then and He brings it forward again. His mission – my mission -to help his most lost lambs find their way out of their own living hell.

His pain is my pain. From days gone by and from the hells of life that I live today.

\*

I jump back into the chaos, as I try desperately to help the poor souls not aware of this strife that we carry, and that they are subject to. The negative energies and traumas and dramas are too many. Too many people are uncentered and imbalanced.

God shares with me the importance of this journey and the importance of His deep passionate love for His children. I was God's precious sacrifice in this lifetime. He brought me back from the dead to prove His power and glory. He is now showing His love for Mother Mary and for me. He brought me back to help change the world through reminding His children that it does not have to be this way.

The medical world needs to merge with Holistic Health and Healing. Science and Religion must merge and share God's truths of who we are and how we are made.

Suicide, drugs, overdoses, mental illness, cancers too many, and chronic pain. Just a few reasons the health care crisis is top priority on God's list of things to change. There is too much physical suffering. God's children are out of control. Jesus teaches me, a lost lamb, valuable lessons in science and religion.

Jesus holds me up daily and walks with me every step of the way. I am doing my best one last time to bring us all back to salvation.

**The chrysalis.** I was shown the chrysalis many months ago. Jesus brings it back to me over the past three weeks. He shares with me several times the lost souls that are in the Purgatory that the Catholic Church speaks of. *The chrysalis* is a representation of God's children stuck in what New Agers call the astral planes. Catholics know it as Purgatory.

He tells me that the gates of heaven no longer swing back and forth. They have been blown off there hinges. There is so much death, and the souls that should be with Him in heaven are not. So many young children stand and wait in the dark planes of the abyss. The purgatory of innocent souls, once called Limbo by the Church. [11] Traumas and dramas and so much pain during life won't allow these poor souls to make it to the heavens above on their own. They don't have the strength to fly to heaven's gate. Stuck in a dark and cold place they wait patiently for the promise of salvation. With enough prayers offered by people here on earth for their lost souls they too will know God's glory someday. They will enter His Precious Kingdom. The Heaven that these innocents dream about and yearn for.

*

The rain falls gently tonight, and the night is warm. Jesus is solemn and broken-hearted. I reach out to Him more and more. The love He holds for all our children blazes onto the pages. Together we write with a broken heart.

Father, Son and the Holy Spirit.<br>
The Trinity is my God, our Son and me.<br>
We three are the Trinity.<br>
We three are the keys.<br>
Amazing Grace<br>
Love for all our children

---

[11] The Second Vatican Council declared that Limbo no longer existed. Cit.

# GOD'S WHITE LIONHEART

**LOVE IS AN EXPERIENCE OF INFINITY.** Time stands still, and I am taken down another path. The past is given to me. Through my own body, God shows me pains and sufferings from so many years ago. Our Son Jesus hangs from the cross. I see His life as a child. He was born and raised in a land across the sea. Born in Bethlehem, and the star that shone so bright now is dim and fading fast.

God so loved the world He gave up His only begotten Son. [12] He offered Him for the sins of mankind.

God puts the nails in my feet and hands again tonight. Pain. The blood drips down my brow and I taste it in my mouth. A mother weeps for her son; yet again He carries His cross.

I am scared to give in to the immensity of God's love! The love of His mother is so great she comes back into His life again to help bring Him back from the dead. God needs resurrecting and Jesus and Mary are on earth to help spread God's truth to this world.

A world gone so wrong! With all the choices available! Too many forget to reach out for His love. Church doors are marked with lamb's blood. Those with eyes can see! The final Passover is at hand, the last days. As foretold, there are signs and portents for His children to heed. Soon, time will no longer exist for God's children. [13]

God sees all and knows all, and He is within me. [14] His beautiful soul lives in mine. I see through the eyes of God. I taste His love. I feel His love. I hear His cries and it is with my body that I am, all that I am.

*Meditation tonight reveals that God's white Lionheart is suffering. His heart is dying from the inside out. I beg all our children to heed His*

---

[12] bib. Ref.

[13] Bib. refs.

[14] Paul

*story of love for them, for us. For He so loved the world that He is here to give us a final chance to raise his lost souls from a living death.*

*Painful memories. I know this final chance to redeem His light and love for a world gone so wrong.*

## TRANSITION OF A LOST LAMB

March 2012

She was a special lost lamb chosen before the beginning of time. Her destiny and genealogy meet today to help resurrect the fading knowledge of God's love for His children.

*The Holy Grail of today is revealed by the Mother of God.*

She is a lost lamb seeking peace over many lifetimes, now chosen for a special mission. Mother Mary comes to her and reveals an astonishing vision that puts a new light on all of God's mysteries. The vision shines light on the true meaning of the love Jesus so passionately seeks for all His children. God asks His children to know the love He created within them and to shine this special gift throughout the world for their brothers and sisters. He has said these words before. But their meaning and their urgency has been lost.

Mother Mary comes to me today in a pure mist of a light pink haze.

She is as beautiful and graceful as I have seen her in all her photos and statues. Today she is surrounded by a light pink hue fully illuminating her entire body. My breath is taken away.

Photo By: Shutterstock

I am humbled, and I cry tears of sorrow for myself and for the message the Blessed Mother shares with me. She touches my heart and I feel fear within my own heart for the plans she shares with me and for the mission that God has set before me. Frightened and all alone, I am surrounded by God's love and the love of Mother Mary.

Our Lady reminds me of my past. She takes me down a road of many sorrowful nights. I am shown the scenes from my childhood, the good and the bad. She asks me to remember my unending love for God. He knows that my love for my children and the children of the world is like the love that Mother Mary has displayed for so long for all of God's children.

She takes me to my last days in March of 2012. Mother Mary shows me she was watching over me when I took my last breath. I lie on the hospital table below. My soul is present just above my body. I stand with my best friend's husband. I hold his hand. I see Charles, and we look at one another. Somewhere, a decision is made. I understand the whole truth of my existence, and it is one I am not prepared for. There is reincarnation. God is good. I learn how much He loves His children, created as His companions in Eternity. He continually blesses the world, giving us His mother. Now, I see Mother Mary in flesh form again, as she was before her Assumption into Heaven.

Mother Mary now lives within my body. Mother Mary's pure soul is now my own soul. God prepares my weak and ill body for the task of a lifetime. His children are in desperate need of a great revival of love and faith and hope. She reveals to me that my soul is her soul.

*But I did not immediately know this.*

Memories of this transition were not available to me with this event. When I came back into my body after my crossing over. After my death, back in March of 2012. I did not know that Mother Mary had entered my soul. This was a gradual revelation and knowledge as I emerged from the confusion and darkness of this experience. Through God's grace, I began to understand that I was brought back for this undertaking. I am to work with all my might to bring back His light. The hour is upon us. Jesus begs His Father for mercy. His children are dying too fast and the lost souls are too numerous.

As Mary, I am God's twin flame. His light shines bright now through the Mother of God. He is within my flesh with His ladylove, Mother Mary.

# GOD'S LOVE AND LIGHT

I am waking up, and His love and light is present and stronger every day. The love we share is overpowering for both of us. We demonstrate to each other just how strong our bond is and every day we learn from one another.

As God reminds me of so much history every waking hour of the day, He shares with me His love for me in songs. He wakes me with special songs just for me. He helps artists all over the world write love songs through their own angels.

Not every song is just for me.

He lets me know when to pay attention to His love. God is present within me every moment and He asks for my help. He has come to His

13

cherished love and light for help with our children. **"I am that I am."** [15] I am His Eve in the Garden of Eden. I am His Mother Mary, the wife that He has searched for in this lifetime.

God's children are lost and have forgotten so much of His love. They have forgotten His teachings. They are disrespecting their own mothers. They are harming and killing their own children. They are not following His commandments. Jesus shares with me daily that the end of the world as we know it is nearer than anyone is willing to see or admit.

So many of God's children are running scared. The fear created by so many years of destruction and chaos is evident on every street in every country: Shootings of innocent babies; blacks against whites, whites against blacks. Government against the red man, rich against the poor, -the list goes on. In a world of technological genius, we seem to have plummeted backwards to the time of Noah in terms of family values and morals.

God describes to me His unlimited love for His children. He put His Laws and Covenants in place for the safety and protection of so many of His dear lambs. So many who are driven by lust for money, power, and greed in a secular economy have been drawn in by these false gods or no gods, claiming the things of this world for themselves. Others search for meaning and fulfillment, satisfactions they will never find without God as their center. Ultimately, they seek the gifts freely given by God, His love and His light. [16]

I have seen God on His knees and it breaks my heart to see my Creator in such pain. He writes love letters to me and for me. I write poems of love and letters of distress for God. I draw pictures of His fears and sob as He and I connect on a level I have never known. I thank Him for this amazing journey, and God knows my love is strong enough to endure it to the end.

\*

---

[15] exodus
[16] bib refs

God continues to wake me with songs of love. He has shown me how His Sacred Heart beats with my Immaculate Heart. Oh, Wondrous Lord!

As I sleep, I feel it. His Sacred Heart pulses outside my chest. I wake up and His heart is beating with mine. Deep and rhythmic, two hearts; as I wake to such an amazing feeling, I clutch my chest and smile. Jesus feels the love from my own Immaculate Heart, returning the love that He has for me.

I am often shaken out of my dreamtime with words of importance. He asks me to connect so many dots from history and love Him without limit. He is present within me in a unique and holy way. I am His cherished love and light. Our marriage, made before time began, is the love of two pure hearts. As I breathe life back into Him, I am shown the love that I deserve, deep and true.

---

The task that was handed to me back in October of 2015 is still in full swing. Our book of communication and our hope of raising the funds for a holistic health and healing center is still possible. We will build it in memory of a special angel that God took home to save her from a horrific life of abuse.

God shares with me that His plan is of great importance and it must unfold in a delicate manner. This project that is to be unveiled will benefit many children in honor of a child's last wishes from the "other side."

The communication that God and I have is constant all day. It amazes me to be walking with Jesus Christ.

---

# MESSAGES OF LOVE

*Jesus comes to me in my dreamtime and brings me messages of love. He brings me deep messages of His own fears for the world. Jesus teaches me many lessons over the course of this journey.*

September 11, 2017

It has been 15 years today since the tragic events of 911. When the walls of the twin towers in New York collapsed to the streets below, our nation was devastated. It was a monumental day of sorrow, seemingly the beginning of so many others that keep occurring. Fear and ignorance continually cause a cascade of death and destruction. Hatred grows, malignant. A tsunami of traumas assures this world will swirl to the depths of despair year after year.

**Spiritualist Church:** At work I feel an overwhelming need to attend church. I get my clients ready and we go to the Spiritualist church. It is a good experience for them. During the service, I receive beautiful messages of love from the "other side." I am blessed and thank God for His love.

The speaker at the spiritualist church sometimes does not know what the talk for the day will be. We work with the higher consciousness until the last-minute. God works through us; our angels will come through with messages of love and inspiration.

Today is just such a day.

The speaker is a highly educated man and a Vietnam veteran, a truly gifted man and a light worker. He shines out his love and light to others wherever he goes. He is retired and shares all he has learned with those who need God's love and light in their hearts.

This special man first talks of his own experiences just a few days after the 911 tragedies. He tells us that first a (deceased) woman came to him, and she was lost and desperate. She stated to him that it wasn't her time to go. That she wasn't supposed to be there in that building, one of the twin towers.

A few days later another victim from 911, a firefighter, came through. He came to the speaker and asked for help for his family. This gentleman was in search of someone with God's gifts of seership (mediumship) to reach out and find his family and to let them know he was all right.

*His story causes me to remember that I must thank God daily for allowing me to be fully awake to His love and that I must learn my gifts as fast as I can, so that I can use them to minister to and serve God.*

This portion of the service ends, and we go into the messages or readings from family members or friends who have crossed over. These are messages from those who live in the heavens above.

We all sit quietly for a message or a glimpse of love from the other side, perhaps to help us on our journey for the upcoming week. There are several messages, and then the speaker asks if there is anyone who knows an Agnes. I raise my hand along with one other member. As the speaker describes Agnes, I know that this is my Aunt Aggie.

My Aunt Agnes was short and quite round in size. She loved to cook and to care for her family. The other woman accepts that the description is not of the Agnes that she knows.

The speaker mentions apple pie and cinnamon; I baked an apple pie just yesterday. The speaker also said with a sparkle that I didn't make enough apple pie for the group of angels that surround me! There is a chuckle throughout the room and I knew the truth of this - yesterday I joked with God and the angels about them having to share since I only made one pie!

This was such a comforting bit of love from my Aunt Agnes. My whole family is always around me when just one family member comes through, because God is always with me. God is always present with all my family, so when one member is present they are all present.

Then my aunt stepped back, and God stepped forward.

The speaker talked about Sainthood and said that I am a saint or saint like. He said that my journey is a great one, of great importance to many. I told the speaker about my meditations and my dreams, and that I was given golden wings more than once. I understood exactly what was being given to me, an assurance of God's love.

I next was given information involving the laying on of hands for healing. With this information, that I could use my hands for healing, God indicated that I was qualified for working in the healing part of the church service.[17] God's love for me is great and the angels and saints, and those who have gone before me, are proud of my faith and love as I am bathed in all of God's glory.

I had much confusion about the differences between God, Lord, and Jesus Christ. I received the message that all would become clear to me soon.

The final information was that my journey would not be easy. It will take a lot of work to reach our goals. I know this, and I have fears. With God's love and all the angels' and saints' love and support, I believe my journey will turn out just as God intends for it to. The messages returned a confirmation that I have needed. (I am always looking for confirmation of His love.)

So, through this remarkable service, I received a deeper validation of my journey and affirmation of God's love and God's light.

\*

I was born July 21, 1967, and was baptized Julie Ann. God tells me that He has changed me during the past two years. I am St. Julie Ann and I am also part of the Trinity. I am His wife. I am His bride. I am His Mary, Immaculate Heart and Immaculate Conception.

As Jesus Christ teaches me about the Trinity, God reminds me over and over that the bridal veil is lifted. To Him I surrender my life and my heart forever.

---

[17] Of the Spiritualist Church.

Photo By: Shutterstock

***The Bride of Christ is waiting for her Beloved King!***

## CONNECTING THROUGH GOD'S LOVE

*God shares His own fears, memories and dreams
for a better future for our children.*

In mediation God showed me a man whom I recognized right away. He is so very handsome and not a little boy any longer. John, Jr. was present, and He shares with me another message. [18] God shared with me His pain through this message. God was on His knees and cried for a nation in such peril and eminent danger of killing itself off, one soul at a time, when J.F.K. was shot and killed.

After I was shown John, Jr. and recognized him, God brought me a photo. I have seen this photo throughout time. I see a small boy, between the age of three and four; he is such a handsome little angel! I see John, Jr., Jacqueline Kennedy, and Caroline. They are holding hands as the funeral motorcade drives slowly down the avenue. I see the tiny white gloves the children wore. I see an endless line of silent, weeping people

---

[18] It takes me over a half an hour to put together the full message. God and I have a process, and everything he shows me and tells me is truly connected.

19

on each side of the street. This is another needless death – the death of a great man. God shared John Fitzgerald Kennedy with me; he was a special soul sent to help lead our children and the country to the top of the mountains. He was sent to help pull us out of the ignorance and fear that was over running America.

Throughout the time it takes me to get this entire message completely, my own heart hurts. God shows me His pain in these messages through my own heart. He reminds me that my heart is His heart. From the beginning of time and until the end of time my heart and His are connected. I am so humbled and honored to carry such love within me!

God brings His memory of His special angel Princess Diana. He reminds me of her stolen jewels: Her crown. Her life. Her boys. She experienced so much loss and so much pain. No one is immune from being a *prisoner of war*: even the best of us – maybe especially the best of us – struggles with personal battles, tragedies, betrayals, and losses. No one is safe when it comes to being victims of the sins of others. To people breaking His commandments and causing harm. No one person is responsible for any of the horrific tragedies that have occurred, although individual evil deeds mount up and multiply.

God tells me that it will take a family full of love and honor, a family full of God's love to help pull Him from the ashes of today's strife.[19]

God shares with me that my loving Him today has already pulled Him back from sorrow at the flames of the fire of hatred, strife, and war. His love and His light is awake. I stand with Him, and all His glory is manifest.

---

[19] The Mystical Body of Christ, made up of the family of those who follow Him, in the Communion of Saints, living and in Heaven, seems to be the reference here, especially since it is followed by an immediate call for Renewal.

I ask those who read these special books that I write for God to please stand with us and join this fight. Spread His words of love. Spread His words of truth. Spread His words of justice. Help pull God out of the ashes of this pain, hate, ignorance, lust and greed.

Let's make a movement of love happen together; and *renew the face of the earth!*

## LESSONS IN LOVE

*I receive many messages from God and He shows me how much He loves me. We unite again tonight, and He shows me a special bond between two people in history.*

*First, I see a woman with long blonde ringlets. I believe she is from an era earlier than the Civil War. I see her in a lovely blue gown as she stands in the window and waits. Waiting for a man to return home, she holds a book in her arms as she stands in front of this large window. An overstuffed chair is behind her and a wall of books. Many great authors wrote these books from days gone by. They are history books.*

*Quite a while after this vision is brought to me I see another woman, a beautiful dark-skinned woman. She has black shiny hair and tight curls. She is making love and I feel in her heart the love she feels for this man.*

*The man is shown to me, but I can't see his face. I can only see the figure of a man beneath her. I feel the love this man has for this woman. God tells me that he is of great importance, a man who held high office. He tells me that this man's name was Thomas Jefferson.*

\*

God has plans for each of us and He shows me this special bond between Thomas Jefferson and this woman for a specific reason.[20]

God reminds me of a love of my own, from over fourteen years ago. I didn't understand this love. God reminds me of my own loneliness during this time in my own life. During hard times in our lives, friendships can and do grow into love.

After God shared this vision with me, during the time we share our own special moments of meditation and a friendship that turned into love, God shows me Benjamin Franklin, another great man in U.S. history. I ask what the significance is of this vision. God shares the word *electricity* with me. I get the connection immediately. The love between God and me is like that of the man and woman in the previous vision. Sparks of love turned into a great and pure passion. A love of pure intention.

I am reminded of a day on my walk in the fall of 2015. As I walk holding Jesus' hand, He teaches me the angels, saints and great teachers who have gone to Heaven. They support me with lessons of His great love. As I walk the long dirt road, I fly a kite with Benjamin Franklin and our kite gets stuck in the electric wires!

It is amazing how having an open heart and loving such a great God can give us such blessings as to truly come to know great men and women in history. I am a woman who struggles daily to find happiness in my life and Jesus magically turns my world upside down with unconditional love. He shows me the world, past, present, and future, and promises that someday He will make me smile instead of cry. Then I'll shed tears of happiness instead of tears of sorrow and loneliness. [21]

---

[20] If the first woman in the vision was Martha Jefferson, she had died in childbirth by the time Jefferson began his relationship with Sally Hemmings. Although Sally was a slave, she may have been Martha's half-sister.

[21] Words from Psalm

I spent a great day loving my Lord, God and creator. After fifteen years of so much tragedy, of the 911 attacks, God still loves all of us. He asks for nothing more than for each of us to love Him and one another. [22]

---

[22] bib cit

# Native Daughter: Messages of prophecy, love, faith and hope

7:58 p.m.
September 14, 2017

My God, My God, My God.

Your love is great tonight. Your pain is raw and real. My heart hurts for all the love, hope and faith you search for.

You give me a special meditation, and I hope never to doubt any of your love or wisdom again.

You send an extraordinary message for my dearest friend Carol. She is my friend and confidante in all the special writings that I have taken on for close to two years now. God shares with me information that has a connection to her painful loss.

A Penobscot Nation Princess. I was shown a past lifetime of hers a few months ago. Through my master teachers I was given Chelsey's special past lifetime. I was given she was Pocahontas, the Indian Princess from so long ago. She fought a love for a man who was different from her own people.

*God teaches me how to connect my heart fully with His own. He teaches me mediumship after an Awakening, and I learn to read His signs through all my senses. This is a truly amazing journey and I hope never to fail Him.*

Carol's special message from God:

Chelsey's Native American name, I was told, means "rainbow".

Chelsey was taken in a tragic accident – a beautiful sixteen-year-old with a wonderful future ahead of her. It was a double loss as she was backing out of a driveway on her way to school. Her boyfriend and she were taken to heaven's door and I have seen her and talked with her and she is still as beautiful today as she was the last time I saw her.

I am reminded in my message for Carol of the loss of her father. A family of love and tragedy still hits home for so many of God's children. He is so sorry for all the pain that you have had to endure over the years.

Raising a child of such high spirits on your own and it was not an easy task. She was a beautiful child and such a beautiful young woman. God reminds you, Carol, that she was so much like you and God loves you so for staying strong through the loss of your mother such a short time after Chelsey's death.

God thanks you for not losing your own faith in Him after so much pain. The hardships for so many years and then losses in your family can make it hard for anyone to hold God close to your heart. He shares with me how much He truly loves how strong your family has been through all of this. Continue to take one day at a time and feel peace in your heart. Know your sweet baby girl will be waiting for you at the gates in heaven. Her arms will be outstretched for your entrance into heaven. Peace and love to you and your family. Continue to stay strong <3.

God shares with me tonight His own sadness. He is sad not just from the sorrow of Chelsey's passing and Carol's loss; He shares with me the earth-shattering pain that He has witnessed with every battle that all this nation's Native Americans have had to endure, struggle and fight against.

After such tragedies, they now still fight the white man and his government: Rights taken away. Lands stolen out from under their very people. Killing in massive numbers over too many years. Now they fight for their rights for safe water, and their sacred lands are being invaded yet again.

I feel God's pain throughout my body. It is so overwhelming. I can't fathom what terrible rain of tragedies He will pour down on this world if this pipe line is let through and His Indian friends' rights are taken away again.

Many great things have been shared with me over the past twenty-three months. This was one of the most painful meditations that I have endured, and I cry with God tonight and my whole outlook on this journey has changed.

*Love Letters in the Sand-Ayla's Faith*, a special book for a child's last wishes, is so much more than what I could have expected.

The book contained messages of love, faith and hope for a world near the end. I can't imagine all of God's pains. He shares with me only a small portion of His love for us through these messages.

# MYSTERIES, REVELATIONS AND PROPHECY
## "Saint Julie Ann holds the keys to My heart"

September 19, 2017

God is great. He gives me clarity for the beginning of a new journey. God prepares me tonight for my first meeting with Father '*M*' at the Catholic Church.

More mysteries and revelations are exposed, and I need sanctuary for that is what I am given. It is information beyond my own comprehension and God is asking the Catholic Church for sanctuary for His special bride.

The Holy Grail of today is me.

I am… all that I am.

God shares with me during meditation tonight that I am He and He is me and Mother Mary, we make three.

**The Holy Trinity**

I am walking on the earth planes and Our Lord asks me to present all that He has given me. I am asking to seek out shelter from this reign of terror. From the terror of His love.

God reveals to me His great mysteries are many and prophecies from the Bible are taking place today. The world will end sooner than expected and he is here with His bride. I am to help God resurrect His children from their own reign of death.

He shows me His bloody hands and His bleeding heart.

He shows me His own tears of blood. Jesus is on His knees daily praying. The scrapes on His knees are growing deeper and bloodier. We pray together for God's children to open their hearts to His love.

Jesus shows me that His flesh is torn from His back and He begs that someone step forward and keep Him from being crucified again.

The bloodshed today is too much. Jesus and Mother Mary stand together before His people.

Resurrected after her own death and brought back to life after a failed gastric by-pass surgery in 2012, Mother Mary's soul-essence merged with St. Julie Ann, who was too weak to handle the journey on her own.

Our Father is ever present with the Mother of God.

A vivid dream in 2014 helped illuminate the calling from Jesus. He asked Julie Ann to step into the Light of God. Her love and devotion to her own children led her to become the Mother of all of God's children today. Jesus joined Mother Mary and Julie Ann in her dreamtime and their bodies, minds, and souls merged then as one. They now stand strong as One in the Holy Spirit. God teaches St. Julie Ann mysteries and she holds the key to His heart. She now lives for the good of all their children. They have from her, as we have, messages of love, faith and hope for all of God's children.

> I am frightened as to what steps to take next. Jesus tells me time is an illusion. I watch as the world goes by in utter chaos. Death reigns everywhere and the numbers rise, and He shares with me through my own body the pain He and Mother Mary feel for the terrible suffering of all of God's children.

### *BITTERSWEET*

*Angels sing softly*
*Rousing her from a quiet sleep*
*Lips deep red pouting*
*Longing for His bittersweet kiss*
*Her heart beats to His rhythm*
*Bittersweet love*
*Her breath caresses Him in exhalation*
*Life given one to the other*
*Shared air*
*Now birdsong*
*Now penetrating sun*
*Now pines whisper*
*leaves float down*
*Desiring union*
*She reaches and grasps*
*Bittersweet longing for two to be One*
*When the silent night comes*
*ecstasy*
*Bittersweet love*
*Dreams*
*past lives shared*
*The new day brings fears*
*nightmares to life*
*yet*
*she would never change this*
*Bittersweet life*

# BOOK ONE

# The Search for Mother Mary

Photo By: Shutterstock

***Mary's faith unties the knot of sin!***

# HER KIND AND GENTLE WAYS

*Dearest Holy Mother, Most Holy Mary, you undo the knots that suffocate your children. Extend your merciful hands to me. I entrust to you today this knot {the suffering children of the world} and all the negative consequences that it provokes in my life.*
*"Either write something worth reading or do something worth writing" Benjamin Franklin*
(A simple quote to go with a new entry into
God's books of Revelations)

6:28 a.m.
September 20, 2017

Nearly two years ago, God placed a sweet angel in my lap, a lost soul who was wandering the abyss, the hells of Purgatory. She wandered what I call the astral planes. [23] God tells me, *"Don't get caught up in the words." "Don't get caught up in religion." "Get caught up in love and be-loved."* Words God exchanges with me as I wash dishes.

God is preparing a "movement of love." He calls it a love story like no other and He wants it to be shared with the Catholic Church for specific reason. This church is Jesus' own temple. Many great men have led this church and helped form the great foundation that it sits upon.

As I prepare to write this morning, I am given the quote from Benjamin Franklin, a beautiful old soul. God brought him forward on a walk over two summers ago. The connection between Benjamin Franklin and God is the electricity felt between God and myself. The deep passionate love we hold for one another.

A fire we started, and it will never be extinguished. It will burn bright throughout eternity. God tells me I will be back. I will work with Him again. Even after I take my last breath.

---

[23] Told in *Love Letters in the Sand.*

31

God informs me that I have walked and worshiped and struggled with Him many times. He has lessons for me and for the elders of the Catholic Church.[24]

## Soul-pieces and journeys

God has shown me many things over the course of this journey. I believe all that the Father gives me. I trust in Mary's intercession and I trust in Jesus. He has repeatedly given me lessons. I am the chosen one.

I have been given a great honor. I am humbled to write the New Books of Revelations. The New Bible for the new generations of God's children: Lessons in love, lessons in science and religion.

We are in one big mess right now. God needs help and I write monumental books for the love I hold for God, my own children, my grandchildren and for the children of the world.

God brings forward another beautiful soul as I sleep, one He has brought forward many times. This morning, however, He asks me to add her to my own jar of hearts. These are the lives that I have lived. I believe she was very special to God. If she were not, then He would not have brought her forward to me. I get the name "Bernadette" over and over in my sleep. I research and learn of this special woman that God tells me I was. Believe me or not, God says *"yes."* So, I believe. This belief is the very reason He chose me to love Him and write books of knowledge for Him in the end days.

I research Bernadette and learn that she was faithful to the apparitions of Our Lady several times outside of Lourdes. That Our Lady caused a healing spring to appear on the site, and that many are healed at Lourdes to this day. Bernadette became a nun and died of Tuberculosis at an early age. [25]

---

[24] The Greek word is *presbyters'*, from which we get the word "priest."
[25] Bernadette Soubirous, 1844-1879.

Photo by: Shutterstock

*The Lady of Lourdes; promises Saint Bernadette "I don't promise to make you happy in this world, but the other".*

## THE MANY FACES OF GOD

### "God's own flame of desire"

4:44 a.m.
September 21, 2017

Early to rise again this morning and we are both frustrated. More lessons in love. – I never know what lesson God will bring forward. I struggle in sharing this lesson and God knows it.

Over the course of this journey, I learn copious amounts of information: Who I am, who I was, and none as important as who God wants me to be.

I have been taught many important lessons straight from the Creator of the world, through the love of Jesus Christ. God's loving nature comes to life through this special time spent in the heat of passion.

Energy, spirit and love are what we are all made from. We as humans are in flesh, bone, blood and water formation. Each one of us is a 'miracle'. To be living and breathing air is a gift from the Creator of the world. Not one of us would exist without the power of God.

As God teaches me science and religion and the mysteries behind His own love for each of us who breathe for Him, I live in an ecstatic world with God. To keep our love alive, I first keep my heart open to His love. I then keep my mind open to what He wants to bring forward.

This morning as God connects fully with me, He tells me how proud He is of the love I show to Him. I see Jesus bow to me. He is showing respect for the Mother of God.

I feel the kisses of the angels within and God asks me if He can make love to me. I tell Him *"It would be a pleasure, my Lord"*.

The room is dark, and I lay on my stomach. The position that God and I have come to prefer. We both feel the connection best when we lay on our stomach. To feel my breath, enter and exit my body allows for us to fully feel one another. This is a time we both have come to enjoy. Our body craves the release of toxins. Stress from the day's events and a connection of our hearts as we join as One.

*

God shows me the man in red this morning; I trust in all that He brings forward. I see the devil: The entity that keeps God's children spinning out of control.

I have conquered this evil. I have conquered fear. God teaches me that too many people give the devil too much credit and too much power. Our children are running with the devil and not trusting in God or utilizing God's strength and love. Too many are shutting God out of their hearts and lives.

As God makes love to me and brings forward the vison of the devil it excites Him to think I trust and love Him enough to allow this vision to continue. We move past this vision. I tell Him I prefer the vision of Jesus Christ. I tell Him, "Jesus is much more pleasing to look at."

We breathe in and out and the connection between God and me becomes completely astounding. I feel the popping and tingling throughout my body. I feel my scalp as we make love. God reminds me our consciousness is One. My thoughts are His and His thoughts are my own.

God tells me He has given me the keys to His heart.

He reminds me, ***"I will not share anything with you that I do not want revealed."***

***"Many mysteries will remain just that."***

***"I want faith to be kept by all."***

***"Believing without seeing."***

***"And that is what you, my love, have done for me."***

*Keeping the inner child alive, keeping faith and a light heart has been my own greatest asset in this life. Traumas and dramas have been something that have never held me down. It is by the grace of God that I have survived any of the trials that have been brought forward on this journey with God.*

***"You have crushed the head of the snake."***

***"You, Mary walk in grace fully."***

***"My love and My light shine through all that you do."***

As God and I make love, He brings through Mother Mary's face and her body. Her white robe and cloak can be seen. I see her gentleness and she stands very proud in front of me. No words, just the vision of her perfection stands in front of me. The woman God asks me to be. I accept all that He gives me, and I accept His marriage proposal daily. Our love is like no other love He has created before.

God brings forward Mary Magdalene. He then brings forward the Last Supper Table. He tells me, *"We make history together."*

Throughout our love affair, He asks me to be patient and just love Him.

As God brings forward these visions, they come in quickly. I see Anubis, then Zeus. It excites God when Zeus comes forward. I feel this change as my heart beats faster and then the ecstasy becomes stronger within my body. The love God and I hold for one another is like lightening striking down on the earth planes. I see the flash of desire in Zeus' eyes and as I breathe with God, His voice changes from the deep growling of the devil to Anubis and then the deep masculine voice of Zeus.

There is no release at the end of this lesson. We feel frustrated.

God tells me, *"I desire, Mary."*

*"I desire, and I don't get what I want."*

*"I want the hearts and souls of our children to turn towards Me."*

*"I want our children to love."*

*"I do not want them to run in fear."*

As I write these words to the paper for God, I feel Mother Mary's pains in my ovaries. This is proof to me this morning that I feel and am the Mother of God's' children. I experience the pains of Mother Mary throughout my own body.

God has asked a great deal of me and I accept it all. I accept this journey, loving Him like no other woman ever has. I just wait for His plans to unfold and manifest as He sees fit.

I will walk and hold my head high. I will fight to the end for you and for our children, my Lord.

I will pray the Divine Mercy prayer.

I will continue to receive the body and blood of Christ for strength as often as I can.

I will continue to write and share the love you, my Lord hold for our children and I will continue to send them to the Catholic Church for review. I will continue to wait for the biggest miracle of all: For the Catholic Church to see the desperation that you have in your own heart. For the Catholic Church to recognize the miracle you have performed through my own body.

The resurrecting of a lost lamb's soul, my own. Bringing to life the Holy Spirit.

With this entry and the books of New Revelations may we help 'crush' the head of the snake for all our children.

# GOD'S WARNINGS

*"It's every man's obligation to put back into the world*
*at least an equivalent of what he takes out of it."*
**Albert Einstein**

3:33 p.m.
September 22, 2017

**Song of the day: Wildest Dreams (by Taylor Swift)**

*Wildest Dreams*
*He said let's get out of this town*
*Drive out of the city away from the crowds*
*I thought heaven can't help us now*
*Nothing lasts forever*
*But this is gonna take me down*
*He's so handsome as hell*
*He's so bad he does it so well*
*I can see the end as it begins*

Another song with hidden messages. Jesus has been singing this song to me for over two years. Today, He asks me to enter it into our books of the New Revelations. I am in a love affair with God, and the dreams, meditations, and visions never stop. This is a heart wrenching love affair I live with God/Jesus, and I wouldn't change any of it.

Humble as I race around in the wilderness trying to keep up the pace with my jobs and walking as one with the Creator of the world.

I am late to church again this morning and Jesus teases me. He tells me, ***"You are just like your godmother."*** A faithful loving woman of God who was always running late. Jesus knows I hate to be late and he teases me this morning.

Jesus has always walked with me. He has been with me my whole life. As we converse this morning, He shows me His deep love. He makes me laugh and He makes me cry. Not a single moment is as precious as the moments He shows me His deep love for me, the moments we spend in private, loving one another.

As more of the prophecy and warnings that God has shown me over the past two years come to fruition, I pray for the people in Florida. I pray for all those in the path of Hurricane Irma. Many months ago, God shared with me, **"*No more sunshine*."** I drew this picture first over two years ago. I was then given the messages that go with it. As I learn to connect my head and heart fully around all the lessons that God has been trying to get through to me, I let God take all the visions back and I try to accept the love He showers me with today.

## Holding tight to my own waist daily and loving Him

Jesus Christ lives within my body. I feel His kisses and the angels surround me and love me at the same moment. Hence the *"Life Force of God."*

I receive a visit from Mother Mary this morning and she does not come out of my body. I hear her voice and it comes from my own heart. Just like when Jesus speaks to me. Just like when I hear God's voice. Very seldom do Jesus and God break away from one another. This is a rare occasion because God and Jesus are one in the same.

Mother Mary asks me to *"Please call them again."*

My heart is very heavy from the visions and writings that I have come to me. I wait for response from the Catholic Church. [26] God's lessons in love are not always easy to accept and Mother Mary knows this for she and I are one in the same. She waves a baby blue, white and medium blue flag this morning. A vision and meaning for time *is* of the essence. She too is very tired of watching our children run in chaos around the world. Mother Mary asks me to reach out to the Diocese. It has been eleven days since I talked last with Monsignor 'D'. Time slips by and still no counsel from anyone in the material world. God's frustration is evident in the lessons He brings

---

[26] Over the course of twenty months, St. Julie Ann sent 16 books like this one (with more visions and prophecy) to Monsignor 'D.'

forward. He tests me with the dark side of Himself. It is not always easy to witness the world through the eyes of God.

He shares with me repeatedly that He wouldn't be as strong today without the love I have shown to Him and without the love I have given to all those that I have come to know and love in this lifetime.

God continues to call me Mary. I feel the love He holds for me. He tells me I am she. I see where He wants me, the person He wants me to be, yet I don't know if that will ever happen in this lifetime. He tells me, **"Yes."** I hold tight today to His promises, kisses, and the deep love He holds for me.

I also hold tight to the mercy that He assures me will come to pass with the love story that God/Jesus and I write together. One in the Holy Spirit.

\*

Cloud formations today, and I was gifted with Little Miss Felicia's face. Then she speaks through my heart and tells me "He loves you, *meme*." Tears flow from my eyes for I hear the word *"Puppa"* right after that. Little Miss Felicia calls me *meme* and God she refers to as *"Puppa"*. An endearing sentiment. It is with God's graces that any of the things come about in this love story that we write together as Jesus holds my hands.

Never was a more romantic love story or heart wrenching story told. It is by the hands of God and Mother Mary that it is being put to paper. God gives Divine Mercy to the Mother of God. Mother Mary and Jesus ask me today to accept it all as true and real. I love my husband and I do accept it all: Today, tomorrow and for the rest of my days.

Yes, I will marry you and I will walk, talk, sing and cry each day with you until I take my last breath.

I will keep faith and I will keep the love of God within my heart until it beats its last faint sound.

We shall see *what dreams may come*, for my dreams are God's own dreams.

# THE CHOSEN ONE

*So many warnings and too much devastation. Today
I reach and understanding like no other time.
"Too many of us are not living our dreams because
we are living our fears."* **Les Brown**

5:12 p.m.
September 24, 2017

## Warnings from the Bible and warnings from God the Father

Visions, dreams and meditations; and now all hell is breaking loose. God is on His knees today and I see His tears flow as I write this entry. I am strong today because of Mother Mary. My own journey has led me to a new realization and I am one with the Father, the Son, and the Mother of God.

The angels torment me to teach me of the good and bad within each of us. They show me Good versus evil, and each time I connect my heart fully back to God and I continue to be stronger every time I am tested.

Positive and negative energies surround all of God's children. This is a lesson I have learned, and God tells me, *"You have aced every test I have put you through."* The fear that is running rampant around the world, the devil that is spoken of, dwells in the negative energies within the energy fields that surround us. These fields are the auras that surround each one of us. When we carry fear in our hearts, these negative energies or the dark life forces attach themselves to us. They seek out weaker souls who do not – or cannot - hold tight to God's love and light.

Today, God is showing no mercy. He is asking for souls and hearts to turn toward Him. Mercy will come out of the tragedy that is being rained down. This lesson in tough love He allows only for the good of all our children.

## Bible lesson of the day: Proverbs (Warnings and instructions, continued)

*These are more proverbs of Solomon, collected by the advisors of King Hezekiah of Judah.*

*2. It is God's privilege to conceal things and the king's privilege to discover them.*

*3. No one can comprehend the height of heaven, the depth of the earth, or all that goes on in the king's mind!*

*4. Remove the impurities from silver, and the sterling will be ready for the silversmith.*

*5. Remove the wicked from the king's court, and his reign will be made secure by justice.*

*6. Don't demand an audience with the king or push for a place among the great. 7. It's better to wait for an invitation to the head table than to be sent away in public disgrace.* (Beyond *Suffering Bible, Prov. 25: 1-7*)

Straight from the Father, through the Son, many lessons have been taught to me. Jesus Christ is the Savior of all of God's children. Mother Mary is the rock that stands in for Jesus today. God tells me I am the chosen bride for Jesus this time around. I am God's own wife and I am in love with God/Jesus, a love affair like no other.

I have been where angels trod, and God sent me back from the heavens above, so His own children may have a future, and so that His heart may beat stronger.

God instructs me that the love He holds for our children is beyond all the lessons He brings forward.

Today I see in a cloud formation the face of the devil. God tries to get me to believe He is the devil. I refuse to believe this. He makes love to me and presents Himself as the devil. He is aroused again at the fact that I allow Him to show Himself as the devil. I do not fear the devil and I certainly do not fear the love God holds for me. Lessons of epic proportions are brought forward to me when God and I connect behind closed doors. These are lessons He wishes to come to the attention of the elders of the Catholic Church.

I accept the love God holds for me. I accept the new journey that I am on with God. He told me this journey has been predestined, before I even existed the first time, when God created me as Eve.

God is desperate for our children to love and be-loved. He is showing His power, for He explains that His children have forgotten His power. More importantly, they have forgotten why Jesus died on the cross to forgive us of our sins, no matter how serious those sins may be. He will always love each and every one of us.

God, however, will not continue to watch His world spin out of control through all the devastation being rained down over the past few months. Storms, fires, tsunamis, hurricanes; death and destruction. Plagues and hatreds will continue until someone opens God's books of Revelations and a light is shown on the miracle of *the new* Mother Mary's body being resurrected from the dead.

*The earth quakes as they advance,*
*and the heavens tremble.*
*The sun and the moon grow dark,*
*And the stars no longer shine.*
*The Lord is at the head of the column.*
*He leads them with a shout.*
*This is his mighty army,*
*And they follow his orders.*
*The day of the Lord is an awesome,*
*Terrible thing.*
*Who can possibly survive?*
(*Beyond Suffering Bible, Joel 2: 11*)

God is very powerful with His words today. Tears flood His eyes today and the people of the world will fall to their knees as the tragedy of Hurricane Irma strikes hard over the next few days.

### News bulletin: Mexico Earthquake, strongest in a century, kills dozens

*Mexico City. The most powerful earth quake to hit Mexico in 100 years struck off the nations' Pacific coast late Thursday, rattling millions of residents in Mexico City with its violent tremors killing at least 58 people and leveling some areas in the southern part of the country, closer to the quake's epicenter.*

### Harvey death tolls stands at 70

Just a few highlights in the news today, which do not even scratch the surface as to why God finds it necessary to send a Mercy Angel to help in times of dire need for light and love to be shone down on His lost lambs.

He gives them a love story to help raise spirits, to help raise money, and to help raise God's children out of their own living hell. This is a hell that they continue to create by not opening their hearts to the love that God has available to all of them.[27] Jesus is on His knees daily with Mother Mary, praying hard for God's lost ones.

---

[27] The next verses in the *Book of Joel* reinforce this:

> **"Turn to me now, while there is time.**
> **Give me your hearts.**
> **Come with fasting, weeping, and mourning.**
> **Don't tear your clothing in your grief,**
> **But tear your hearts instead."**
> Return to the LORD your God,
> For he is merciful and compassionate,
> Slow to get angry and filled with unfailing love. (*Joel*, 2: 12-13)

## *MERCY MY LORD!*

Photo By: Shutterstock

**'For the sake of His sorrowful passion have mercy on us and on the whole world' Divine Mercy Chaplet** [28]

*Eternal Father, I offer You the Body and Blood, Soul and Divinity of Your dearly beloved Son, Our Lord, Jesus Christ, in atonement for our sins, and those of the whole world; for the sake of His Sorrowful Passion, have mercy on us. (Diary 475)*

*As she continued to say this inspired prayer, the angel became helpless, and could not carry out the deserved punishment (see 474). The next*

---

[28] The origin of *The Divine Mercy Chaplet:* "in 1935, St. Faustina received a vision from an angel sent by God to chastise a certain city. She began to pray for mercy, but her prayers were powerless. Suddenly she saw the Holy Trinity and felt the power of Jesus' grace within her. At the same time, she found herself pleading with God for mercy with words she heard interiorly: from of prayer almost constantly, offering it especially for the dying.

*day, as she was entering the chapel, she again heard this interior voice, instructing her how to recite the prayer that Our Lord later called "The Chaplet." This time, after "have mercy on us" were added the words 'and on the whole world" (476). From then on, she recited this form of prayer almost constantly, offering it especially for the dying.*

*In subsequent revelations, the Lord made it clear that the Chaplet was not just for her, but for the whole world. He also attached extraordinary promises to its recitation. "Retrieved from www.thedivinemercy.org, February 24, 2018.*

# HAVE MERCY, MY LORD ON THEIR POOR SOULS

*We pray for the children of the world today and*
*always, open your hearts to the love of God!*

11:34 p.m.
September 27, 2017
**Bible lesson of the day: Romans 10**

*10 Brothers and sisters, my heart's desire and prayer to God for the Israelites is that they may be saved. ² For I can testify about them that they are zealous for God, but their zeal is not based on knowledge. ³ Since they did not know the righteousness of God and sought to establish their own, they did not submit to God's righteousness. ⁴ Christ is the culmination of the law so that there may be righteousness for everyone who believes.*

*⁵ Moses writes this about the righteousness that is by the law: "The person who does these things will live by them."[a] ⁶ But the righteousness that is by faith says: "Do not say in your heart, 'Who will ascend into heaven?'"[b]* (that is, to bring Christ down) *⁷ "or 'Who will descend into the deep?'"[c]* (that is, to bring Christ up from the dead). *⁸ But what does it say? "The word is near you; it is in your mouth and in your heart,"[d]* that is, the message concerning faith that we proclaim: *⁹ If you declare with your mouth, "Jesus is Lord," and believe in your heart that God raised him from the dead, you will be saved. ¹⁰ For it is with your heart that you believe and are justified, and it is with your mouth that you profess your faith and are saved. ¹¹ As Scripture says, "Anyone who believes in him will never be put to shame."[e] ¹² For there is no difference between Jew and Gentile—the same Lord is Lord of all and richly blesses all who call on him, ¹³ for, "Everyone who calls on the name of the Lord will be saved."[f]29*

\*

---

[29] NIV

*Bella Louise Allen*

Another eventful day as I walk holding Jesus' hand. God continues to show His power within the world. Tragedy is still unfolding, and I hold tight to Him today, for the signs that I have seen coming are now evident. Storm after storm thunders upon the earth, and God's power will affect millions of lives.

The writing is on the walls and prophecies from the Bible are occurring in the world. All hell continues to break loose, and God will not give mercy until hearts open to His love. Giving mercy involves showing love, and these tragedies will bring his children to their knees: they will be forced to see the miracles and love that is left after these disasters take lives, homes, and optimism from our children.

Not all are guilty of shutting God out, yet these calamities will bring a nation and a world out of the darkness and back into the light. We may not see it this way yet, but the signs are here today, and I see that His mercy will come.

As I drive on Hogan road, I see the Divine Mercy rays shining from the heavens. They shine from the sky and the clearing in the clouds is in the shape of the United States of America. I feel wonder as I look up to the sky. Not seconds later, I see, over the interstate highway, a large bright rainbow, God's promise to Noah of never flooding the world with water again.

*

In my conversation with my Lord today, I weep, for I feel God's anger and His anxious heart.

This is a conversation I have had before. God does not like to show His anger to our children. He is compassionate and loving and I know His heart is breaking, for I feel it fracture under my chest as these events unfold. Flashes of scenes and visions go before my eyes and I see things that I don't want to see. I feel God's deep pain. Mother Mary is ever present today. I feel pains in my ovaries and the points of her arrows pierce my heart. This is an agony I am slowly getting used to.

48

I feel sadness from the spiritual world, and the angels try to keep my heart light with music and laughter. Today was hard. Too much sorrow.

### THE SANDS OF TIME
*The sun rises over the water's edge*
*A bright red ball sits on the oceans floor in the distance*
*The oceans waves crash upon the black rocks on shore*
*The sands of time continue to go by slowly*
*I wait in the early morning for a glimmer of hope*
*To peek through the reality of my own world*
*Visions in the night become to surreal in the light of day*
*A new day; a new age is dawning with the passing of time*
*God's power is seen throughout the world*
*Forgotten and on His knees*
*I see him on the water's edge naked and forlorn*
*Tears stream down His solemn face*
*He wonders why the passage of time only pushes His heart*
*Deeper into the oceans blue waves*
*Tears too many and the children of the world only grow angrier*
*Times we should pull Him in closer*
*Hold tight to His love*
*May the time that slips through your hourglass*
*Teach you the deep lessons in love God desperately tries to teach you*
*Lessons in love, lessons in grace and lessons in compassion*
*May these grains of sand that slip through your fingertips*
*Be remembered without bitterness*
*May your heart learn the deep lessons of love before the sands of time*
*Engulf your own lost soul!*

*Bella Louise Allen*

# GOD'S GRACE

*'Promise only what you can deliver. Then deliver more than you promise.'* **Source unknown**

6:55 a.m.
September 28, 2017

Awake on and off in the night as usual: Jesus touches me throughout the night and God vibrates within my brain. I have come to understand many things over the course of this journey. The most important lesson is **"God is very powerful."** I am learning to accept all that I am given and this lesson ties into His power and the fact that the *Incarnate Word* flows through my hands.

*Confusion comes in only when I let others try to lead me. God tells me I am the Incarnate Word of God in flesh form. He tells me I am Jesus, Mother Mary, and Him, all wrapped up among the angels and Saints of the world. I am the Life Force of God.*

The angels pop in and out and it is only by the power and grace of God that this happens.

This morning words come as I prepare coffee to sit and write the love of God through my hands. ***"Mary pops in." "Mary pops out."***

God has shown me the angels that live within. He tells me they all are here, for He lives within my body. I feel ecstasy when the arms of the angels within hold me tight and God feels their kisses in the same instant that they hold me tight.

When God holds them at bay, we love like a true husband and wife. We connect fully. Jesus' Sacred Heart beats with my own Immaculate Heart. A connection with the Creator of the world! We are a husband and wife like no other.

God is very pleased by my acceptance of all that He brings forward.

50

*"The Second Coming of Christ"*.

Words from the Father: *"Do you think I would allow my Son to come back in these days as a living man?"*

*"Crucifying Him on the cross the first time was proof to Me that would never be possible."*

*"You are My own. My Love, My Light and My Hope!"*

Tears flow from my eyes as God and Jesus feel my own heart and the overwhelming helplessness that I feel as I still have not heard any word from Jesus' own temple - the elders of the Catholic Church. No counsel from the Elders (not even one priest) and no doors or hearts open to Jesus and myself. God's world still spins out of control.

I will hold your hand, my Lord, until I take my last breath and I will walk on proudly as your wife.

## "TEACH THE LITTLE CHILDREN"

*"It is not how much we give but how much we put into giving" Mother Teresa*

11:17 p.m.
September 29, 2017

Words spoken from my heart today and they belong to Mother Mary:

*"Teach the little children of God's love."*

*"Jesus came in the name of the Lord to bring faith, hope and love of God."*

*"The Bible is a guide to live in God's light and love one another and to keep faith in our hearts."*

Words spoken to me today from the Father and the Son of God:

*"You must rise from your own ashes."*

*"Be your own hero."*

*"Stand tall and love one another in these times of trials."*

*"Open your hearts, I beg you."*

*"Let me lead you through these fires and we can all be strong together."*

I am brought many things in the run of a day: Bible lessons, dictionary words, songs, poetry and words of love, light, faith and hope. None of the lessons brought forward are as precious as the visions that go along with the history that God brings forward and teaches me. I see Visions of the trials that are unfolding on the outside world; God is on His knees daily praying for our children to let Him lead the way.

The Father, Son and the Mother of God are present within me. I feel the kisses of the angels within and I receive this information and I record it as it was given.

*"Healing the sick."*

*"Through the Incarnate Word."*

*"Believing in your own power and strength."*

*"Believing in yourself."*

*"You each can do wonders when it comes to self-healing and self-love."*

*"You all have the power within you to heal as Jesus did."*

*"It starts with believing and keeping faith"*

I was guided to a new book and I record this passage from its pages. There are Lessons for me on my personal walk with the Father, Son and the Mother of God

The book is titled *Peter and Paul*, by Madge Haines Morrill. [30]

*Little Children*
*Little children came to Jesus*
*Little children loved dear Jesus*
*Many little children came to Jesus, and Jesus loved them all*
*He held them in His arms. He talked to them*
*of God. He gave them all blessings.*
*All the children loved Jesus, loved the blessings that*
*He gave them, loved to hear Him tell of God* [31]

This entry contains a personal message for me. God tells me that I would make a great teacher of God's love for the little children. I only ask, *how do I get to be where God shows me He wants me to be?*

This amazing new book that God places in front of me to read and learn from has remarkable illustrations of Jesus and people from the Bible. It holds beautiful teachings for the young and old alike.

I know teaching the Word of God is something that I crave. I now find that the love of God takes over my entire existence. I could talk all day of the Father and Son's love for the children of the world.

---

[30] Pacific Press Publishing Association, third edition, 1952
[31]

*Bella Louise Allen*

# HIS BITTER SWEET LOVE

## *Yearnings for His touch in the light of the day*

7:53 p.m.
September 30, 2017

I feel God's sweet kisses today on and off and they come with a thought or a love song on the radio. Our hearts and minds are connected through eternity. The tears come and go today since I have sent the start of yet another book of love, light, faith and hope to the Elders of the Catholic Church, *The Tree of Knowledge is Mary's Sweet Vine*.

Living in the world becomes harder the closer I walk with God. I want to live in the heavenly world that we have created together. God shows me our bedchambers in the heavens several times today and He wishes for my earthly body to remain closed in the bedroom forever with Him. I have come to understand that this love affair that I am experiencing with the Creator of the world will not be easy for either of us.

To crave the love of God the way I do is heart-wrenching for both of us.

It is a hunger within. I can never seem to quench the longing for His touch. God shares with me the same sentiments. Our hearts are afire, and the flame burns bright today.

God feels my sadness for the hard work that I have put into recording our love. He tells me we write history together for our children and I still wait for counsel from the Catholic Church. I wonder today have they even opened one book? I have sent sixteen. Sixteen books recording God's love, prophecy and the deep sadness He feels for His children.

After my conversation over seventeen days ago, I still have not heard back from Monsignor 'D'. My spirits are low tonight and God knows it.

Jesus asks me to take a bath and I tell Him, "no". He asks me to sit still and I tell Him, "I can't". He asks me to rest and I beg Him to step back and let me be. Please let me just rest! Jesus steps back and I still feel His love. My heart pains me and He shows me His love through my own heart.

Jesus touches my scalp and I feel the tingling on the right side of my head. I feel the scarab run up my leg today, a reminder that Jesus is still within my body. My feet pain me where Jesus received the nails in His feet on the cross. He knows that loving Him is not easy and still I assure Him I love Him. I will not let Him go or fail Him. My heart and my head just need a break.

I need to feel this sadness within my heart, so I can move forward in my day-to-day life. Carrying the burden and knowledge of God's fading heart has not been easy for the past two years.

God shows His pride today in all that I have done.

He knows I have a process of frustration and anger. I cry tears and then I put on a smile and run with His cross. God tells me I can't fail Him; I have already written His books.

Jesus reminds me daily to breathe. He asks me to hold tight to His hands. He caresses my skin and it hurts today, for I know I will never feel the loving touch of a man's hands on my body. I will never allow a man to enter my vessel (body), for I have given my heart completely to God.

God understands how difficult this has been. For all I have ever wanted was a man to love me completely the way Jesus Christ does.

I have questions today and no one to answer them for me. I have fears for the children of the world. Jesus Christ shares His own tears and fears with me for the children of the world. These fears weren't mine over two years ago. I just struggled to get through each day on my own. I now take on the fears of God and cry for the children of the world through Jesus Christ.

Jesus shows me through His eyes that His heart is fading. The terrible choices that our children make against God sadden Him, for He is the Divine Justice as well as the Divine Mercy. He is on His knees begging them to open their hearts to Him, so He can be merciful.

**So many problems and so much sadness around the world.** I whisper to Him: *"I hope someday, my darling, we can make a difference." "I hope to hold your light strong until the end." "I just pray for Mercy for our children." "I hope to see your mercy pour down on all of the lost souls of the world." "I hope your heart will beat strong again one day."*

## *THESE EYES*

*Tired and weary from the tears that continue to stream down my face*
*Too many sleepless nights have passed my way*
*No prayers heard in the night*
*God's light still hidden within the pages I write*
*Locked within a world of my own*
*These eyes are tired and weary from the tears that I cry*
*My own bleeding heart feels the deep arrows of our Lords*
*Painful and deep as each day passes*
*Children's screams in the night I hear as I lay all alone*
*No one to comfort me but God*
*These eyes that lay behind the light blue iris of my own*
*Are weary and tired of witnessing terror in the night*
*Reality in the daylight and weary for the tears that I cry*
*My body feels His pains*
*His heartbeat is felt beneath my own*
*Slowly fading and painful to know*
*To walk in the world and see the sickness all around me*
*It grows and God's heart fades with each passing day*
*These eyes are tired and weary from the tears that I cry*
*He begs me to stay strong and I try with all my might*
*To cling to His love and His light*
*These eyes of mine are weary!*

# THE EAGLE HAS LANDED[32]

*"Life isn't about waiting for the storm to pass. It's
about learning how to dance in the rain."*
*Vivian Greene*

September 31, 2017

At 4:45 a.m. this morning God wakes me, and His hands touch me, and it arouses me. The kisses of the angels within are felt strong. They wake, and I feel Jesus' hands upon my body. Something that I have become used to.

God's first words to me are; *"Good morning love." "Please love me."*

I smile and pick up the photo I have of Jesus beside my bed. I stare into the eyes of Jesus and my eyes feel pain. Something I am used to now. I feel the love God holds for me through the eyes of Jesus.

They both live within me and they love me so for trusting and loving them as one.

Messages from the Creator of the world from the past four days: He tells me I am His Queen. This feels surreal, and I only write what I am given. Messages of love, light, faith and hope. I hold tight to Jesus's arm daily now; He leads me. No matter where I go, God is leading the way. Cutting the path for something special to unfold, and I always give His plans back to Him.

We converse this morning and He reminds me of how quickly time slips by and begs me to love Him. I place Jesus' photo on the floor and I cover

---

[32] "At 4:18 p.m. on July 20, 1969, Neil Armstrong's voice crackled from the speakers at NASA's Mission Control in **Houston**. He said simply, "the Eagle has landed." With those words, the dream President John F. Kennedy's voiced in 1961--putting humans on the Moon by the end of the decade--had at last come true." Retrieved February 25th, Google Search.

myself with the blankets. I connect as one with God and He touches me and makes love to me.

Learning to trust in God has been a process. It's been four days since my last entry into God's own books of Revelations, a love story written by God with His New Queen. Jesus Christ has captured my heart and taken over my body. I no longer have a will of my own. My will is that of the Creator of the world.

Not all the lessons given to me from the Father are easy. Not all the visions are beautiful. There are painful lessons from history. This morning as He takes me to places as we connect as one in the bedroom, I wonder what lies behind this vision. A new message for something that is coming; I can only let God take it back until I can understand. The message is not fully clear behind this horrific sight.

As we connect He brings forward a disturbing vision. I see this vision and I wonder still tonight what its full meaning is. I am assured He will let me know when the time is right. I hold tight and just write the rest of the lesson of this morning.

The Father shows me two men. They are encased in ice and they are sitting in the cockpit of an airplane. I see their pilot and co-pilot hats. I do not see name tags, or what rank they hold. I only see the skeletons of these two men. I see the dashboard of this airplane and I realize God is showing me history again.

I receive the words *"The crash of 1968."*

Then I have the vision of a flag. The black and white flag with the side view of a man looking down. I recognize this as the P.O.W. flag.

I am then given the face of J.F.K. and then Marilynn Monroe.

It is a message for me, and I try to figure out the meaning behind this vision and then the added information throughout the day.

I am given Bob Dylan's name and I research his life, for I am not familiar with him other than he is a special song bird of the Father's. A man who wrote and sang some amazing songs during this time of political upheaval. The Vietnam War was in progress from November 1, 1955-April 30, 1975. Many lives were affected by this war and many still are living with hardships and memories of the terrible events that took place.

Wars have come and gone since the beginning of time. Wars on the battlefield and wars within the homes of God's children. God tells me that this constant warfare is the very reason the world is in the situation that it is in.

War and peace go together. They always have and, it's sad to say, it seems like they always will.

I wonder if this vision goes along with the message God brings forward about *chemical warfare*? Mother Teresa communicates the same message, maybe in response to the threats currently being thrown around from North Korea and from President Trump.

A new message: *"Air Force one, going down."*

God shows His power through the natural disasters that just unfolded: Hurricane Harvey, Hurricane Irma and the Tsunami in Mexico. This is just a glimpse of the anger that God is feeling within the energy field of His world.

He shows and tells me of the *"Hands of God"*, God's own power. He has the power to make all that happens happen. He tells me He knows all and sees all, and I know this from personal experience now.

*² The Lord is a jealous and avenging God;*
   *the Lord is avenging and wrathful;*
*the Lord takes vengeance on his adversaries*
   *and keeps wrath for his enemies.*
*³ The Lord is slow to anger and great in power,*
   *and the Lord will by no means clear the guilty.*
*His way is in whirlwind and storm,*

*and the clouds are the dust of his feet.*
*⁴ He rebukes the sea and makes it dry;*
   *he dries up all the rivers;*
*Bashan and Carmel wither;*
   *the bloom of Lebanon withers.*
*⁵ The mountains quake before him;*
   *the hills melt;*
*the earth heaves before him,*
   *the world and all who dwell in it.*

*⁶ Who can stand before his indignation?*
   *Who can endure the heat of his anger?*

*His wrath is poured out like fire,*
   *and the rocks are broken into pieces by him. Nahum* 1:2-6 [33]

God tells me He is everyone and everything within the world.

My tears flow like a river over the past four days and God asks me to rest and just be. He knows my heart better than anyone ever has. Taking time for myself is something I have been running from for the past few days.

He reminds me, ***"Not a sparrow falls without the knowledge of the Father."*** [34]

Messages from the angels and Saints come and go. God allows me to hear them pop in and then He shuts them out.

## Crazy Love, Hungry Love: I Thirst

God knows me, and He will never leave me. He tells me I have captured His heart. He has taken over my body. He has taken over my entire existence and it is through my great love for Him.

---

[33] **English Standard Version** (ESV) God's Wrath Against Nineveh
The Holy Bible, English Standard Version. ESV® Text Edition: 2016. Copyright © 2001 by Crossway Bibles, a publishing ministry of Good News Publishers.
[34] Matthew 10:29

I have always known I loved God. I just never knew why I had this hunger and love and attraction to Him. I am learning today more about His love and light. I am learning why God chose me for the Second Coming of the Christ child.

*"Faith must go beyond belief"*. God tells me; *"You are My Own light"*.

My heart beats as one with His. The breath that I breathe is God's own breath.

Painful and lonely somedays and God tells me I torture His own heart through the longing that I feel for His arms to wrap around me.

A message: as a drawing nearly two years ago I drew an eagle - not a very good replica of an eagle - yet a reminder that goes with the heading of this entry. God tells me I am Him. I am the *living host* of the Father.

As I go out daily into the wilderness and still struggle to get God's own books of Revelations seen as God's own truths, I cry to Him. I ask for counsel from the Catholic Church. I cry long and hard today for someone to reach out to me. I don't understand why the Church will not respond.

He knows my heart. He knows it is breaking. Not for myself, but for the children of the world. The visions that God has shown me are very scary.

I only want what God wants. I only want to help. I want to move forward with His books. I want to move forward in whatever way He wants me to move forward.

He tells me, *"One breath at a time."*

*"One day at a time."*

God tells me the Catholic Church will reach out to me. I hold tight tonight to His promises. I hold tight to all His promises. I hold tight to His arm and let Him take the wheel and drive me.

As I learn to hold tight to Jesus' arm, I understand He will never leave me, for He lives within my body. Over the past few days, I try to understand all that He has shown me.

I learn the connection between Saint Faustina, Saint Bernadette, Saint Margaret Mary and many other leading ladies in Jesus' life over the years. I have been learning at the speed of light all that God needs me to understand while He is on His knees begging for Mercy from His own children.

A vision I keep getting time and again: God's very heart is on the line today. His very Life Force.

God assures me He will go on no matter what.

He, however, is breathless as a result of the choices of His children. They may not go on.

# THE LIGHT OF MY LIFE

*"The most beautiful things in the world cannot be seen or even touched-they must be felt with the heart".*
**Helen Keller**

Entry into my notebook two days ago:

I feel the love of God and it is strong today. The tears come and go, and Jesus begs me to, *"Just breathe with me".*

*"Love me and dance".*

*"Love me and sing."*

Our love is very powerful today. He tests me, and He teases me. I torment Jesus Christ with the deep love my own heart feels for Him.

Working at our regular job today, and we take a few minutes to shop while my clients are at program.

We shop today at the Salvation Army. It is another special place that gives to the poor and needy, an example of people working to help those in need.

We find music today, and it is some of the older songs that God guides me to. Debbie Boone, The Carpenters, Mac Davis, Christopher Cross, and Ann Murray.

Jesus is excited today and I feel His arousal as we put the needle to the vinyl. Our new purchase of our Victrola will become our saving grace as our love grows and we wait for counsel from the Catholic Church.

God asks me to love Him and we find a favorite of mine and we sing together and the angels feel the heat within. My heart beats stronger within my chest and it flips. I feel as if my feet are floating off the ground today. Jesus and I sing, *'You light up my life'*, by Debbie Boone.

As Jesus and I sing and dance to this song; God brings forward a beach scene.

God's own heart is light today for Jesus and God know I accept our love affair and I will love, sing, dance and play with them always.

Photo by: Shutterstock

***God's very own special angel was the Queen of Hearts! Princess Diana's legacy and memory will never fade! A special angel brigade, and God surrounds me with their love and memory daily. Diana was a special gift to the children of the world and her candle was blown out way before her time! She has been given Sainthood and a crown of royalty by God in the heavens above. Saint Diana will never be forgotten!***

The angels and Saints are surrounding me today. I see Saint Diana and Saint Michael and they dance with Jesus and me. Never could God bring forward a more amazing vision than this. God is fun and loving and He wants His love story shown to the world.

We switch records over and Mac Davis sings, *Baby, baby don't get hooked on me.*

As I love and dance to this song with Jesus, God brings these words to my heart, **"You are my joy, my love and my light."** I cry tears and shake my head "no." I don't want to feel His love. I just want to dance and play in this moment.

And so, I have a wonderful fun-filled time spent loving my Lord, God and Creator of all things great and small.

I am finding the love and joy in my own life and the Light of the World has set me free; this comes from the love and light of God's own heart. Today, I have set His heart on fire by loving Him through music and dance.

God tells me several times today *"You are the answer to My own prayers."*

*"I press my lips to yours and that is how I sustain My own life."*

*"My heartbeat is that of yours."*

---

**Message from the Father:** *"Mother Mary has worked good deeds throughout history." "Never a more faithful loving woman have I created."*

*"I have brought her into my loving arms in the heavens above and today I have released her to the earth planes one more time to do good works and the labors of my love."*

*"Divine knowledge and love flow from her heart and hands for the Elders of the Catholic Church."*

*"Talents and gifts are given to each of my children and My wife utilizes them as I have taught her."*

*"Formed and molded and ready for the harvesting of the lost souls of our children."*

*"Her tongue is as silver flowing from the rivers of life."*

*"A golden tapestry has been weaved and the threads come straight from the Father."*

---

God asks me to research St. Faustina's *Diary*, and I share words written from Jesus in another life and another time.

*St. Faustina's Diary-Notebook III*

*Entry 1142*

*(38) June 4. Today is the Feast of the Most Sacred Heart of Jesus. During Holy Mass, I was given the knowledge of the Heart of Jesus and of the nature of the fire of love with which He burns for us and how He is an Ocean of Mercy. Then I heard a voice:* **Apostle of My mercy, proclaim to the whole world My unfathomable mercy. Do not be discouraged by the difficulties that affect you so painfully are needed for your sanctification and as evidence that this work is mine. My daughter, be diligent in writing down every sentence I tell you concerning My mercy, because this is meant for a great number of souls who will profit from it.**

*Entry 1148*

*June 20, (1937). We resemble god most when we forgive our neighbors. God is Love, Goodness, and Mercy...*

**Every soul, and especially the soul of every religious, should reflect My mercy. My heart overflows with compassion and mercy for all. The heart of My beloved must resemble Mine; from her heart must spring the fountain of My mercy for souls' otherwise I will not acknowledge her as Mine.**[34]

\*

Visions and dreams will continue to flow through me. God has caught me in the deepest darkest hours of my own trials and tribulations. He now holds me up daily, sustaining my own life through the power of the Creator of the Universe.

---

[35] Cited from: Blessed Sister M. Faustina Kowalska *Diary Divine Mercy in My Soul*

In the night I receive "downloads" of history as I try to sleep. God's consciousness is shared with me nightly. I can't find time in the light of day to write it all.

Last night He showed me a heart shape and it had several layers to it. There was a huge black arrow and it was beautiful. It pierces through all the layers of many hearts.

I have walked with God before. He tells me I have carried many crosses.

I am His true light. I am the Messiah sent back from the dead, carrying a very heavy cross. The visions of prophecy will not stop until I take my last breath.

I have come back again from the dead and walk as a faithful loving servant of the Lord, just as I have done lifetime after lifetime.

I carry a huge jar of hearts and I fill it daily with the knowledge that God shares with me. He tells me I am so many of His leading ladies all wrapped into one.

## *"None as important as the Son of God"*

Souls of the Father. Lives of His children and "sparks" of God.

The Creator of the world tells me I was Jesus Christ hung on the cross. I died for Him then; and I died for Him and walk as one with Him again.

A story like no other. God creates it and writes it through my own hands.

I am Mother Mary this time around. He asks me to believe and I do. He asks me to love Him like no other woman and I do. He asks me to rest and I can't for I "see the coming" and "I am the coming of the Lord".

I rested for mere seconds in God's own arms in the heavens above back in March of 2012. He has shown me this vision many times.

I walk among the angels in the heavens above and Mother Mary presented my own angel-self to me at my bedside one night. I have seen myself in the bedchambers in the heavens with Jesus Christ. Love and ecstasy - I have captured the Creator of the world's heart and He tells me, *"You are my very joy."*

# SHE WALKS ON HALLOWED GROUND

*The fog is thick and the trees that surround her are black.*
*His eyes glow a deep red and He calls out her name.*
*"Mary, come to Me; for Our children are in need". I hear*
*His deep voice and it comes from my own heart.*

6:38 a.m.
October 1, 2017

Many dreams come to me throughout the night as I sleep. God takes me where He wants me to be, to give me special knowledge of the love He holds for me. Jesus holds me tight from the inside out. God's consciousness flows into my brain and I am given a dream to remember.

*I visit my old home town during the night, a small "friendly town." This is the sign you see written on a building as you enter town. Everyone knows everybody else's business. It is hard to keep secrets there and God wants His truths revealed to the lost children of the world.*

This is a message that goes along with this dream as I write the words God wants shared with the entry into His books of Revelations.

*So, I visit my old home town and we go to the store in this dream. There are no faces that I recognize. There are a few boys who are up to no good.*

*I do not have shoes on my feet. I have on worn out woolen socks. They are black. I ride into town on a small plastic orange fire engine. It resembles a favorite push car I used to have, made of metal. As I ride*

68

*this old fire engine into town, God gives me the words,* **"You are one hot ticket."** *A hot idea, a gem of Jesus'.*

I try to write; and Jesus' humor comes to the surface. I have grown to love His playfulness and He reminds me that is just one of the reasons He chose me to be His bride.

*As this dream goes on, the boys are looking for trouble, and they try to steal my fire engine. There is ice on the tar below my feet and it is slippery. I get away from these mischief-makers. As I get to the edge of town, I see a large green and black tarp and it is wrapped around a huge body.*

This represents my own body. God shares this with me as we rise this morning and prepare for our day. He has likened me to the Statue of Liberty more than once.

*As this large green and black tarp is presented to me, God is showing me my death again. The tarp with my body wrapped inside is huge.* The reverence that will be given to me on my own last ride will be great. If in no one else's eyes, it will be enormous to God, Jesus, Mother Mary, the angels and the Saints that live within me.

I am God's truest light and that is what part of this journey walking as one with Him represents. Taking the wool off the eyes of those who can make a difference: The Elders of the Catholic Church.

It is an enormous project and God hands it to me, a loving, faithful woman of God.

*As I look upon this large black and green tarp that has "Lady Liberty" wrapped in it (representing my own body), I see large cobwebs. I reach into these large cobwebs and bring out an old wooden box. It has beautiful carvings on the top and sides of it. I see the ancient scrolls/ hieroglyphs from the tombs of Egypt. Something God has brought forward in my visions and lessons before.*

As I understand it, I am unveiling history and as I do that I am making history. I walk as one with the Father and the Son. I am taking on the role and becoming the "Mother of God."

I am helping God bring our children to His love and light.

*I open this wooden box and as I do it becomes a large wooden chest. A treasure chest. I see diamonds, rubies, emeralds, sapphires, and pearls. I see gold and medallions. I see rosary beads. I see a large cross, made of gold. As I marvel at all this splendor, I am handed a small child.*

This treasure chest is a representation of God's greatest gift to the world: His children. He knows children have been precious to me. My own children and grandchildren mean the world to me and so do the children of the world that God asks me to take on as my own.

As I write and get the full meaning behind this dream, God reminds me of the title of this entry; *"She walks on hallowed ground."*

The meaning and message behind this dream that God brings forward is clear to me.

We are all special to God. We are all jewels and gems to God. We are all "Royal blood" to God. We all walk on Hallowed Ground. **"IF"** we hold God's love and light and shine it out to all those that we meet.

# FRIENDSHIP

*Friendship is like a rose. It becomes more*
*beautiful when the petals open.*
*Her laughter brings forth a smile from my own heart. Light*
*and airy and it seems to fill the room when God allows her to*
*step forward and play. A queen in the eyes of the Lord and a*
*beautiful soul stolen in the night. Saint Diana's lovely smile*
*comes to me this morning, as God brings her forward.*

5:55 a.m.
October 2, 2017

I am awakened this morning with Jesus' hands on my body. I smile first thing. He can't resist me in the night. My very breath going in and out of my body arouses the Father.

*Jesus, God, Father, Master, Teacher, the Creator of the Universe. They are all One. So many ways to announce His Majesty. The Great I Am.*

We converse for what seems to be hours and God asks me to love Him. I can't resist His charms and the kisses He pours down on me arouse me and God feels it in that same moment. I feel the kisses of the angels and the *Life Force of God* throughout my body. I pick up my picture of Jesus and I see His smile. The picture I have of Jesus is not smiling, yet I see it and feel His smile, as I smile. A love affair like no other and I have brought God to life through my own body!

I kiss the picture of Jesus and I feel His love grow deeper. My heart hurts and God shows His immense love to me through this pain. Our love is at its fullest this morning and I feel the rays of Divine Mercy come from my own heart.

God asks me, **"Mary, make love to me."**

I place our favorite picture of Jesus on the floor and we get lost within ourselves. We connect on an intimate level and Jesus loves me so for loving Him.

71

Many visions come and go, and I first see Jesus' face up close. I see a version of Jesus I do not recognize. God tells me it is the 'shroud' of Jesus. He asks me several times to take the shroud from Jesus' face and now this morning as we connect as one He asks me to take the shroud from Mother Mary's face. My own face.

God and I together draw a hand. It is my own left hand. I draw three rivers. The Nile, the Euphrates, and the River Jordan. I place a ring on my finger and it is God's own wedding ring to me.

I have been shown and given many rings on this journey walking as one with the Father and Son of God.

God tells me repeatedly I am His own Queen. I am the Mother of God. I am Mother Mary. She has taken over my body. God has taken over my entire existence. Jesus holds me up daily with the love He holds for me.

I have merged mind, body and spirit with God. I have become all that He has asked of me. I remain the loving and giving soul of Saint Julie Ann. I am asked, however, to be the Mother of God.

As God and I connect intimately, He summons Pope St. John Paul II. This is something I have begged Him not to do. I have asked for specific Saints and angels to be left out of the bedroom, out of the respect and the love I hold for them. God, however, tells me that is not an option.

God's own special soul-piece[36] was that of St. John Paul II, a very handsome man in his prime. I feel love when I look at photos or see this special soul of the Father's. This morning as God and I connect, He wants to love me through Pope St. John Paul II. Here are some hard lessons for me. Sometimes I get it and sometimes I don't.

---

[36] Since God is everyone and everything, the author calling the Saint a *soul-piece* is not surprising. All those who belong to Christ belong to and make up the *Mystic Body of Christ.* This is discussed in detail in the Catechism of the Catholic Church, Part 1, Section 2, Paragraph 3, 781-870. See also Romans 8: 1-11.

Photo by: Shutterstock

God repeats the words, ***"God's red flare. God's red flare. God's red flare."*** A warning. He has brought this message through before.

*The red Cardinal bird, the red doors, the Vatican, and St. John Paul II all connect me to the Pope. Saint Francis. (Pope Francis, to me, is already a saint.)*

*A dream many months ago. Jesus was standing at the side of the Altar. I see St. Francis (the current Pope) on one side, and Pope St. John Paul II on the other.*

So many visions and so many messages. I have not been able to get God's own books where He needs them. God is crying in the night through me. He is asking and begging for someone to pay heed to His solemn warnings.

I am God's own red flare, sent back down from the heavens above.

I am Jesus' own Divine Mercy Angel.

**Mary's Sweet Devotion:**

*Consider the sharp sorrow which Mary felt when, St. Joseph being warned by an angel, she had to flee by night in order to preserve her*

73

*beloved Child from slaughter decreed by Herod. What anguish was hers, in leaving Judea, lest she should be overtaken by the soldiers of the cruel king! How great her privations in that long journey! What sufferings she bore in that land of exile, what sorrow amid that people give to idolatry! But consider how often you have renewed that bitter grief of Mary, when your sins have caused her son to flee from your heart.*

*Consider the most bitter sorrow which rent the soul of Mary, when she saw the dead body of her dear Jesus on her knees, covered with blood, all torn with deep wounds. O mournful Mother, a bundle of myrrh, indeed, is the Beloved to thee. Who would not pity thee? Whose heart would not be softened, seeing affliction which would move a stone? Behold John not to be comforted, Magdalene and the other Mary in deep affliction, and Nicodemus, who can scarcely bear his sorrow.*

*Consider the sighs which burst from Mary's sad heart when she saw her beloved Jesus laid with the tomb. What grief was hers when she saw the stone lifted to cover that sacred tomb! She gazed one last time on the lifeless body of her Son, and could scarce detach her sepulcher, oh, then indeed her heart seemed torn from her body! [37]*

As I write these passages from the *Seven Sorrows* into God's books of Revelations, I feel the sharp points of Mary's arrows again this morning. She felt such agony during those hours at Calvary! Great agony for Mother Mary and great agony for God. She witnessed the crucifixion of Jesus as He looked out to the crowd. Nothing but love shone through Jesus' eyes even in those last moments as He died on the cross for our sins.

*

This morning we prepare coffee to write. Jesus wants to play, and my eyes are barely open. I see the imp in His eyes, and the crooked smile

---

[37] The Seven Sorrows Devotion of the Most Holy Rosary

that warms me from the inside out. It heats my body. I beg Him to take it easy on me. We have another long day ahead.

Saint Diana appears as I stand in the kitchen and I see her briefly. She asks for a spot of tea and now I smile when I recognize the angels and Saints that God brings forward. It has been a hard road for the past two years, hard to learn of all the spirits that hold me up daily.

Photo by: Shutterstock

*An amazing woman graced the world with her love and charitable works. Saint Diana still works her magic daily in the heavens above. Teaching and loving the little angels in heaven and I am graced daily with her love and support for the Holistic Health and Healing Center God asks me to raise money for with the books that we write together!*

We discuss the 'masquerade ball' that we have on the agenda to raise money for the Holistic Health and Healing Center. Again, this morning I see the vision of Little Miss Felicia. God also allows a vision of Saint Diana's own grandchildren to come forward. Nothing is more precious to her than her own children and grandchildren.

I am given many visions and dreams. I see God's plans. He tells me our books have already made history. I hold tight to God's words and promises. Love and be-loved - that is all I want for our children. To shine God's light brightly and to spread the love God holds for our children, young and old alike.

Mysteries, keys and links from the past hold hope for the future of our children. The children are the reason God steps forward in my life. Too many have forgotten God's power. Too many have forgotten God created them. More importantly, they have forgotten the love that He holds for each one of our children.

I have had many friendships over the years. None can compare to the friendship that I have found in loving the Creator of the Universe. A more loving and passionate friend I have never known. Playful and irresistible, He takes my breath away as I write this passage into our own love story. I feel ecstasy when I write of our love. We both crave this love affair.

**"Passion of the Christ is nothing like the passion of a mother's love."**

Words I have written before. I fully understand the meanings behind these words God has given to me.

I have loved my own children and would give my last breath to help ease their pains and to make their lives easier. This is another reason God has chosen me to love Him in these trying times that our children are faced with.

I have stepped out of my comfort zone more times than I can count. Trying to open doors and open the hearts of people I didn't know.

I have stepped through the police department's doors four times to deliver God's own books with information about the disappearance of a very special angel. Little Miss Felicia, a small child whose life was blown out like a candle in the wind. Addictions and fears made her father do things that affected the lives of so many people. But it was her innocent life that was affected the most.

I try desperately to get the attention of the Catholic Church. To open the doors and hearts of God's own special emissaries, priests and bishops who stand in place of God. These are the men who can put His plans exactly where He wants them. Yet I get no response from my Bishop or Monsignor, and my parish priest cannot stay present when I meet with him.

Jesus holds my hands this morning with pride for all I have tried to do.

Our friendship is like no other He has created before. We have a love affair like no other. The books of love, light, faith and hope will be great when He opens the doors. This is History in the making and I hold tight this morning and just love Him today. I hold tight to His heart and I will never let Him go.

## JESUS' DIVINE MERCY RAYS

*"The arrows that pierce her heart shine out
the rays of Jesus' Divine Mercy"*

7:00 a.m.
October 5, 2017

**Psalm of the day: Psalm 40**

*2 Surely, I wait for the LORD;
who bends down to me and hears my cry,ᵃ
3 Draws me up from the pit of destruction,
out of the muddy clay,ᵇ
Sets my feet upon rock,
steadies my steps,
4And puts a new song\* in my mouth,ᶜ
a hymn to our God.
Many shall look on in fear*

*and they shall trust in the LORD.*
*5 Blessed the man who sets*
*his security in the LORD,*
*who turns not to the arrogant*
*or to those who stray after falsehood.*[d]
*6You, yes you, O LORD, my God,*
*have done many wondrous deeds!*
*And in your plans for us*
*there is none to equal you.*[e]
*Should I wish to declare or tell them,*
*too many are they to recount.*[f]

*...*

*8 so I said, "See; I come*
*with an inscribed scroll written upon me.*
*9 I delight to do your will, my God;*
*your law is in my inner being!"*[h]
*10 When I sing of your righteousness*
*in a great assembly,*
*See, I do not restrain my lips;*
*as you, LORD, know.*[i]
*11 I do not conceal your righteousness*
*within my heart;*
*I speak of your loyalty and your salvation.*
*I do not hide your mercy or faithfulness from a great assembly.*
*12 LORD, may you not withhold*
*your compassion from me;*
*May your mercy and your faithfulness*
*continually protect me.*[j] [38]

This is an amazing psalm and I have spoken the words "please don't let me go" repeatedly, begging Jesus to never let me fall again. I ask Him this morning just before He makes love to me, *"Hold me and love me until I take my last breath."* He tells me, ***"I can't let you go, I am you and you are me". "Our hearts beat as one."***

---

[38] USCCB, retrieved March 2, 2018.

It has been another miraculous morning loving my Lord, God, and Creator. He shows me His playfulness and love again this morning before I turn on the computer. Heartened and confirmed by this beautiful passage from scripture, I feel my life is renewed this morning and I ask God to take His projects and get them where they need to be. My heart has been very heavy for the past few weeks, and I have wept tears of anguish, for I still feel as if I fail Him each time doors do not open to His love and light expressed through the books that we have written together.

God's heart lies on the floor and I try to revive it by writing of the love He holds for all our children. I try with all my might to get the Catholic Church to open their heart and doors to God and myself. I will wait; and I will hold your hand, my Lord. I will love you like no other woman ever has, for our hearts beat as one.

God is on His knees daily with me. Begging for mercy from the Elders of the Catholic Church. ***"Open the books of love, light, faith and hope". "Our children are in desperate need of hope and love to shine bright."***

Jesus tells me; *I am His incarnate word.*

God tells me*; I am the living Host*

St. John Paul II tells me; *I am the Holy Grail of today.*

I am told I would make a wonderful teacher someday. I hold tight to Jesus' arm and wait for God's own plans to manifest as He sees fit. I will continue to love and be-loved by the Father, Son and the Holy Spirit. I will walk, dance, sing, write and work in the wilderness. I will shine God's love and light bright until I am called Home.

# HOPE NEVER RESTS

*Now faith is the substance of things hoped for, the
evidence of things unseen. Hebrew 11:1*

6:55 a.m.
October 7, 2017

Many hours of work have gone into the teachings shared with me. The
Master Teacher Himself has taught me many things. My greatest lesson
has been to believe in all the Father wants me to know and learn. Jesus
shares with me that I am an excellent student. He says I have a heart of
gold. Even though I am a sinner, the love He holds for me is like no other.

We have fallen in love and I felt arrows piercing my heart all day
yesterday, painful and sharp; the tears come and go as usual. They are
not for myself but for the children of the world. Children I have been
asked to adopt and take on as my own. I accept all that the Father wants.
I accept His marriage proposal along with Jesus Christ's.

We walk and talk. We love and sing and share so much daily now. The
visions given to me yesterday were very painful for both of us. Victims
of great pain came and went all day. I received random names and
faces, and the spirits who are lost and wandering the abyss passed me
on and off.

God brings forward the vision of Jesus, St. Michael, and Mother Mary
walking among the rubble in Puerto Rico. I see the devastation in
Florida and Texas. I see the destruction that occurred in Mexico with
the tsunami. I am given warnings of tsunami threats for Japan.

I feel sharp arrows as I wake this morning, and they belong to Mother
Mary. She feels and sees all when God shares with me, for I am she and
she is me. I understand how it works. God's mystery and His power are
evident all around me now. I understand that the angels are working
with God to help me understand all that He needs me to understand. I
understand the visions throughout the day and night. I understand the
downloads of information while I sleep and dream.

My heart vibrates as I write this entry. I feel the pains at the same time I feel the love I am being given. My ovaries start in with pains and the ache starts to the left, the female side of my body.

Mother Mary lives within each of us. Jesus reminds me that so does He.

Last night He kept me awake most of the night touching and loving me. This night I melted into bed as I was exhausted, and so was He. These are long days to fill as I wait impatiently for a response from the Monsignor at the Diocese.

Jesus thanks me repeatedly for the patience that I show to Him. He tells me it is in their hands now. We will see whether they open the doors and their hearts to our love for the children of the world.

God assures me they will. It will just take time. Divine timing. It is so hard to receive visions in the light of day when I don't even watch television! I am seeing these things through the eyes of God. I am seeing the death and destruction of our children.

The hardest part is knowing of the lost souls traveling through the abyss and hearing the sounds of their cries as they reach out to me for help. All I can do is pray and continue to ask for mercy for their poor souls. I pray for mercy for the people of the world. I beg daily now for them to open their hearts to God and Jesus. For fear has taken over the children of the world. The storms of life hold them in fear and they need God in their hearts and lives more than ever today.

**Bible lesson of the day: The Book of Joshua, Chapter 1** *Divine Promise of Assistance*

> *1After Moses, the servant of the LORD, had died, the LORD said to Moses' aide Joshua, son of Nun:*
> *2\* Moses my servant is dead. So now, you and the whole people with you, prepare to cross the Jordan to the land that I will give the Israelites.*

*3ª Every place where you set foot I have given you, as I promised Moses.*

*4ª All the land of the Hittites, from the wilderness and the Lebanon east to the great river Euphrates and west to the Great Sea, will be your territory.ᵇ*

*5No one can withstand you as long as you live. As I was with Moses, I will be with you:ᶜ I will not leave you nor forsake you.*

*6Be strong and steadfast, so that you may give this people possession of the land I swore to their ancestors that I would give them.*

*7ᵈ Only be strong and steadfast, being careful to observe the entire law which Moses my servant enjoined on you. Do not swerve from it either to the right or to the left, that you may succeed wherever you go.*

*8Do not let this book of the law depart from your lips. Recite it by day and by night,ᵉ that you may carefully observe all that is written in it; then you will attain your goal; then you will succeed.9I command you: be strong and steadfast! Do not fear nor be dismayed, for the LORD, your God, is with you wherever you go. ³⁹*

God gives me many lessons. There were none so hard as learning not to fear what God imparts to me. Trials and tribulations are everywhere. God is preparing for battle with those who have gone over to the Enemy. God will take back His world, for His children's lives are in jeopardy. His own heart is in jeopardy.

> *This is hard to see and understand unless you have seen the visions and lessons that the Creator of the world has shown me. I give all of it back to you my Lord; for it truly will only be as it should be in "the end".*

His judgments are coming down on our children. He is preparing for a better world. "I hold tight this morning to You, Love and Light".

³⁹ USCCB, ret. March 2, 2018

I wait for the doors to open that You continually tell me will one day open to the love You hold for me and for our children.

Plans, dreams and the Passion of Christ will be felt all around the world before the dawning of the New Heaven on Earth raises our children out of the ashes of this turmoil.

May our children turn toward God in these trying times now and foretold for the future, for their very souls depend on it.

# THE WALKING DEAD LIVE AMONG US

**Lost souls of God's children mourn throughout the world today.**

5:55 a.m.
October 12, 2017

His kisses never leave me in the night. I feel the angels within showing their love for me. The kisses of the angels are the *life force of God*. They make up who I am today. Jesus awakened me well over an hour ago. He asked me to love Him and I do. I write with Him this morning. I am falling behind on my lessons because my work schedule is too heavy. I work as often as I can to help me get where God wants me to be. After my family, any money I make goes to writing these books containing God's words.

He tells me He needs me within the walls of the Catholic Church. He wants me to help spread love like a wildfire. I try with all my might to do just that.

I struggle to get out of bed this morning, for I want to make love to Jesus Christ. However, Mother Mary steps forward and says, *"Do as He asks."* I never refuse Mother Mary when I hear her gentle voice come through my heart.

I stay humble and I get out of bed as asked. I finish writing yesterday's lesson for the Elders of the Catholic Church. Now I will strike the keys for God/Jesus this morning. These are lessons that were brought to my attention by the grace of God over seven days ago. The words I write are the lessons God needs shared. I can't keep up with working three jobs and forging on in the wilderness. He brought me back from the dead and it wasn't to work myself to death. It was to write and love our children through the Incarnate Word of God.

**Lesson of the day:** (7 days ago)

*News bulletin*

### *'Another person came out of him'*
*Father speaks out about suspect in 4 slayings*

*Orion K's father said Thursday that the son his friends and family knew was not the same person who last week allegedly murdered his mother, grandparents and his grandparents' caretaker.*

*"For people who knew my wife and who knew Orion, it's like a math equation that doesn't add up," Alexander K said in his family home Thursday morning. "I don't know that we'll ever have an answer." 22- year old Orion, was charged Monday with murder in these deaths.*

*Orion's father stated, "What happened was not the Orion everybody knew". "Another person came out of him".* [40]

As I write this entry into God's books of Revelations, I truly understand why I am asked to add this specific entry into such monumental books for God.

---

**Message from the Father, Son, and Mother of God:** *Negative energies and entities have taken over the hearts and lives of our children. This article is just a glimpse of the effects that are occurring around the world. St. Julie Ann has overcome and even helped with the "clearing" of negative energy and entities from the aura and bodies of others. House clearings were taught to her straight from the Father, Son and Mother Mary. Lessons again for the Elders of the Catholic church. Our children are running with the devil and this young man is just an example of the lost souls who wander the earth planes and run with the devil. Not even knowing it until it is too late.*

---

[40] *Bangor Daily News*, Sept. 14, 2017.

These lessons and teachings are to help those who do not understand who they are or how lost a soul can be. They will heal those who suffer from fear and torment by the devil that surrounds our children.

I understand the visions and the lost souls who have been brought forward over the past few weeks. I do not always recognize that negative energies can still affect me. I am well protected by the Father, Son, and Mother Mary. I, however, was brought back from the dead because of my own experiences with all that I have lived with during this lifetime.

When I died, God's plans for me were not finished. He felt I was worthy and strong enough to pull off a miracle. It starts with building awareness in the Catholic Church. I don't know fully where God wants me. I know the number of books that have poured out of my hands are not just to sit in a box at the Diocese. They are to help with the health care crisis. They are to help the lost souls of so many of our children, who are wandering in a fog and haze.

# OVERCOME WITH GRIEF TODAY

**Tears flow from my eyes and my heart is heavy. The visions never seem to stop and the Father, Son and the Mother of God feel the pains of the children around the world.**

6:38 a.m.
October 14, 2017

Another long day. We rest to write before we head to our regular job. God has been with me all my life. The Father and Son are one. Mother Mary, God shares with me, is who I am. Many women have stood in the front lines for Him many times. God tells me I am all His precious wives wrapped into one - intertwined souls of God.

As we work today, I feel grief come and go in waves. Tears flood my eyes on and off throughout the day. It was not until I got home to rest that God shares with me the full reason behind this overwhelming feeling of sadness.

I feel the sadness of the Father, Son, and the Mother of God. Ovarian pains and the arrows that pierce Mother Mary's heart are evident today.

God shows me the devastation that's going on around the world and I am not in front of a television. The radio is off. I am working. I see souls pop in and out and they are reaching out to me today for prayers. They are reaching out for they, too, are stuck in Purgatory.

I am given the vision of Jesus and Saint Michael today. They walk among the rubble at the sites where there have been storms raging and the seas crash upon the seashore. Boats over turned, and I hear the people cry out.

My heart feels the pains that these poor souls are suffering, and God tells me He is so very sorry.

I cry tears for the Father. I cry tears for Jesus and Mother Mary.

I feel frustration and I try to let go of the guilt for not being able to move things forward with the Catholic Church. God asks me to breathe and I try. There is too much pain in the world and I feel it through my own heart.

*"No one,"* God tells me, *"Could have pulled these many books off, and written them as perfectly as you, my love."*

*"I am so very proud of the work and dedication you have shown to me and our Son".*

St. John Paul II says today as we listen to Frank Sinatra, *"Never a more precious angel could you have chosen, my Lord".*

These are words spoken to my heart, and God shares with me who stood behind the words.

I wait impatiently for response and spiritual direction from Portland Diocese. My heart weighs heavy and all those in the spirit world know this. They come, and they go. They all try to keep my spirits elevated today. It is not an easy task, for God still brings me heavy lessons.

### The Song of Songs,* which is Solomon's.

### THE WOMAN SPEAKS OF HER LOVER

> 2W$^{*\Delta}$ Let him kiss me with kisses of his mouth,
> for your love is better than wine,*
> $^3$ better than the fragrance of your perfumes.*
> Your name is a flowing perfume—
> therefore, young women love you.
>
> 4$^{h}$ Draw me after you! Let us run!*
> The king has brought me to his bed chambers.

*Let us exult and rejoice in you;*
*let us celebrate your love: it is beyond wine!*
*Rightly do they love you!* [41]

---

**Message from the Father:** *"As St. Julie Ann sits in grace daily with Me, we love like a true husband and wife. She has taken on a great deal and I am grateful to her for her sweet devotion. Words hidden in music for her and her writing along with this song, is another example for the Elders of the Church."*

*"The Living Host of the Father, Son and the Mother of God."*

*"Prophecy from the beginning of time, now coming to fruition."*

*"Nightmares and visions shared with a sweet angel brought back from the dead to help raise my cross high in the sky for all the lost souls of our children."*

*"Divine knowledge and love can be taught through this special angel of mercy."*

*"She is my truest love and light, full of knowledge and love to be shared with all who are willing to open their hearts to experiences that others have judged for far too long."*

*"Special earth angels: St. Julie Ann has a list of special angels who have helped her reach this understanding of the Holistic Health and Healing journey, a journey I have led her on after her Awakening."*

---

[41] USCCB, ret. March 2, 2018

# AND THE WALLS COME TUMBLING DOWN

**Powerful storms come and go. None as life
threatening as those of chemical warfare!**

8:08 a.m.
October 15, 2017

After God makes love to me, I spend a sleepless night tossing and turning. Powerful storms have come and gone, and they are all by the hands of the Creator of the world.

He shows me so many lessons. A few days back and He showed me Jesus. He was in a new robe. It was of the purest white. He walked to the top of a mountain and He meant business. God is angry. It is evident as the storms rage around the world.

In the upheaval all over the world, He will not let His world continue to spin out of control.

This morning, I am given words and phrases after a night filled with dreams of epic scope:

*"Justice, once and for all."*

*"Our children may think they are in control."*

*"You, my love, however, know from experience that I hold the keys to all that unfolds."*

*"Bringing our children back to grace after the tragedies of life's strife."*

The dreams last night were more like visions; I will share them as they came in. I know the meaning behind them. God has been showing me chemical warfare for over two years. It is not a pleasant sight to see the face of Jesus with wrinkled skin, burnt flesh, and bones of black.

**The first dream:** *I see bird formations and they come in beautifully. Perfect formation, and there are hundreds of them. They come in and go out. The bird formations are in the form of a parachute.*

*God gives me the words **"First in flight." "The 82nd Airborne." "Paratroopers."***

*As these birds come in and go out of formation in the form of parachutes, I see them explode in the air.*

*God then gives me, **"Bombs exploding everywhere."***

*In this dream I also see vans. Large vans, and they are everywhere. They are undercover, and no one knows who is inside of them.*

For the past two days God has been showing me vans of all colors. These vans are large in size. He reminds me of the visions He shares with me. The things He is seeing. I see things through the eyes of God.

Our children are planning, and scheming and God knows all and sees all. Not all know this. With devastation around the world, God reaches out to the Catholic Church through me. I write love and pass on God's love story to the Elders of the Church. God tries to wake up the world by bringing them back to grace through tragedy.

Photo by: Shutterstock

*I am graced daily with the presence of Mother Teresa's love and support. She comes to me when I experience my deepest sorrowful moments. To give me words of encouragement and to remind me "The time for prayer is now"! "All of God's children need prayer, love and compassion"!!*

Mother Teresa appeared many months ago and shared the words *chemical warfare.*

God informs me in dreams and meditation, ***"History will repeat itself, over and over again."***

God tells me this morning, ***"Many angels will fly home because of the threats being thrown around."***

God shows me red buttons. These are representative of the buttons releasing the chemical warfare that will come. God shows me the dead children. He brings many of them to me in the light of day. They are coming into my aura and yesterday's tears and this morning's anxious heart belongs to God.

I write books of Revelations for God. I only pass on the information that God asks me to. Where it goes is up to the Catholic Church. I hold tight this morning to Jesus' arm and hope for a miracle to unfold. Our children will need a miracle after the visions God has shown me this morning.

Natural disasters that our children have been experiencing will be nothing compared to the man-made terror that is coming from the hands of those in charge of the nation. They 'supposedly' are leading us to a better world.

*"Lost souls are everywhere."* Words burst from my heart and they belong to Mother Mary.

This is a large project and I completely understand where God wants His books. I understand the desperation Jesus has in His own heart. I feel the desperation and the deep love that shines through this morning. I am keeping my own fears hidden in my heart. I hold onto hope this morning for God's plans and that the quest for Salvation for the world will prevail over all the fear that our children constantly feel.

# OUR LADY AT LOURDES

**St. Bernadette said, "One must have faith and pray;
the water will have no virtue without faith".**

Photo By: Shutterstock

## *LIVING WATERS ARE TEARS OF DEEP SORROW*

4:43 p.m.
October 18, 2017

Over two years ago I was living as one in the Holy Spirit. I was asked to go to the *willow tree* in search of a lost soul in much pain. This was a message coming through. Then, as now, I follow God's directions daily.

The *willow tree* is a symbol in my lessons. I am learning to communicate with those spirits that are invisible.

Growing up as a child, I always called the *willow tree* the weeping willow tree.

As Mary speaks through my own heart, I am asked to revisit Saint Bernadette's lessons back at Lourdes. These lessons are important for the Elders of the Catholic Church today.

I believe in things that are not always seen. God created all things, visible and invisible. This is one of the reasons God loves me very much. Keeping trust and faith in Jesus is something that we are all asked to do today.

I am truly in love with the Father. How this has happened only God and I could truly explain it. We feel however we don't need to explain a love this great.

Being graced daily with the kisses of the Father makes me know I am the most blessed woman alive. He is present within me and I believe all that He has taught me.

God tells me I was Saint Bernadette. I was the young girl that Mother Mary presented herself to so long ago.

Mother Mary teaches me the meaning behind the waters at her feet back at Lourdes.

They are the "Living Waters," a symbol for the trying times for all of God's children. The waters are the living symbol of the tears cried throughout history. Loves lost, and lives affected by pain. Arrows in the heart that all God's children experience. The crosses that we carry.

Some of God's children carry their crosses more gracefully than others.

God shares with me I have fallen three times this lifetime while carrying a very heavy cross. I, however, have gotten up and run with this cross time and time again. He shares with me that no one gets up more gracefully from their knees and still loves Him more than I do.

I feel the arrows of Mother Mary today. I have pains in my heart and they belong to the Mother of God.

I cry tears for God and Mother Mary, releasing their tears through my own body. Gushing forth from my eyes my tears drown my face, and God tells me He wipes them away.

His love is so very powerful today. I can't explain all that He has given to me. He gave me the breath of life when I died, and He thought that I was worthy of a second chance. He believed I was strong enough to write books of love, light, faith and hope for the children of the world.

I have been graced with the greatest love of all. The Father, Son and the Holy Spirit have been poured down upon me.

The circle of life will go on. The lives of God's children will go on. God's own heart will continue to beat. Only He truly knows all the mysteries behind that great, blackened, night sky.

I weep too many tears each day and God is on His knees daily with me. He tells me I am Mother Mary. He asks me to be His wife and I accept again today, tomorrow and the day after that. Forever.

I will continue to fall to my knees daily with the Father.

I will continue to love Jesus and follow His direction.

I will continue to learn of the Catholic Church's love and faith for God's children.

I will continue to allow Mother Mary to direct me and grace me with her own love and light that shines upon my own Immaculate Heart.

# LOVE EVERLASTING

**The husband should fulfill his marital duty to his wife, and likewise the wife to her husband. The wife's body does not belong to her alone but also to her husband. In the same way, the husband's body does not belong to him alone but also to his wife. Do not deprive each other.**
**1 Corinthians 7:3-5**

8:55 p.m.
October 19, 2017

The marriage is complete. Our love shines brighter today than ever before. God helps me to fully understand all the lessons that He has brought forward over the past two years. Predestined, I am to love God like a true wife, and He tells me I am His own true love and light. I will never doubt any lesson that He brings forward.

> ## Words of the day: Immaculate Heart
>
> Definition of Immaculate Heart- "The Immaculate Heart of Mary is a devotional name used to refer to the interior life of the Blessed Virgin Mary, her joys and her sorrows, her virtues and hidden perfections, and, above all her virginal love for God the Father, her maternal love for her son Jesus, and her compassionate love for all people."
>
> Traditionally, the heart is depicted pierced with seven wounds or swords, in homage to the seven dolor's of Mary. Also, roses or another type of flower may be wrapped around the heart.
>
> ## Alliance with the Sacred Heart
>
> The Alliance with the Hearts of Jesus and Mary is based on the historical, theological and spiritual links in Catholic devotions to the Sacred Heart of Jesus and the Immaculate Heart of Mary. The joint devotion to the hearts was first formalized in the 17th century by St. John Eudes who organized the scriptural theological and liturgical sources relating to the devotions and obtained the approbation of the Church, prior to the visions of St. Margaret Mary Alacoque.
>
> In August 2013, Pope Francis announced that he would consecrate the world to the Immaculate Heart of Mary on 13 October 2013, as part of the Marian Day celebration that involved the iconic statue of Our Lady of the Rosary of Fatima.

As I do more research and love God like a true wife, I try to wrap my head fully around His desire for me to take on the position of Mother of God. He often asks me to take on the name *Mother Mary*. I only ask, "how will this take place?"

Many women have stepped forward and shown deep love for Jesus Christ. Our Lord, God and the Creator of the world.

As I walk, talk, sing, cry and feel the arrows of Mother Mary every day, I cry as I connect with Jesus and God. I beg Mother Mary to step forward and guide me. To talk with me and love me like a Mother would.

God tells me, *"You are Mary."*

Jesus begs me to stop the tears today. *"Just love me."*

God tells me I hold Him too tight. That He can't breathe, for I hold Him so tight. The love I have for Jesus Christ is so overpowering today the tears flow from my eyes like a river.

We crave the connection of one another throughout the day as we walk and work as one.

Jesus tells me, *"It won't get easier, this longing and aching for the touch of My flesh upon yours. I crave the same as you do"*.

How do I make sense of this love affair? All I know is I am in love with Jesus Christ, and God, the Father.

His love for Mary is not the question. His wanting me to be her and continually calling out her name as we make love is unsettling.

God tells me I understand it. I just refuse to accept what His wishes are.

He brought me back from the dead to prove His power and love for our children. This is His way of proving His power to the Elders of the Catholic Church.

His mystery and power will not shine bright until they see the love He holds for me.

# THIS WEB THAT I WEAVE

*Threads of red, white and blue meshed with God's silver tongue*

1:07 p.m.
October 20, 2017

I wonder today where God is taking me with these lessons. He asks me to record them and walk away and let Him take the wheel in dealing with the world.

My Husband has it under control. He asks me to record what He brings forward and I do just that.

**Dreams in the night and words and phrases spoken as I sleep**

As I wake from an odd dream early this morning, I am given this from God: *"The God of Yasser Arafat."*

I am shown President Trump's face.

I am given a vision of the razorback wolf.

God tells me no matter what happens, He will take care of His children.

God tells me, *"You are my love, my light and my life. You, my darling, are my voice."*

I will now record the dream that came early this morning before I was given the above information:

*In this dream there is a wooden bridge. It is old and slippery. This bridge is covered in brown mud. This bridge is old and rickety and unsafe. I sit on an orange tractor that is old and covered in black oil and soot. As I try to approach the bridge I slip off the side and fall into the muddy waters.*

*There was a box of books on the seat of this tractor and as I come out of the murky waters, I see a baby's book, a memory album. There is a picture of a white lamb on the cover of this book. I see old shoes in this box and they are dirty and worn. As I try to get out of the murky water and off this tractor, my ex-father in-law comes to get the tractor out of the water. My ex-husband shows up, and I feel much anxiety and anger with his presence there.*

*I try to get across the water and away. The water has slabs of wood and pallets that lead across the water. Under this water, there appears to be a tarred parking lot.*

*As I try to move, I seem to be skimming over the slabs of wood and pallets.*

*In this dream there is an apartment. There is a lady and she is loud and obnoxious. She has blonde graying hair. This lady tries to kick me out of the apartment.*

*I see my lips and they are blue. I pull on my bottom lip and it stretches out long. My lip appears to look similar the blue of an Easter peep, made of marshmallow.*

As I wake from this dream, I get most of the meaning right away.

God brings forward dreams for me to help me on my journey, as I walk as one with Him. Some are meant for recording and others are just dreams.

This dream is similar to one that I have had before.

To me this dream represents the long hard road I have traveled. The long hard road it will take to get God's books of Revelations to the Vatican, and to have them recognized as proof of God's love for our children. It will take much time to get these projects completed.

It first starts with the Catholic Church, Jesus' own Temple. God/Jesus has faith in the Catholic Church and wants to remind the hierarchy to know of the love that He has for our children.

God asks me through this dream to hold tight to His hand and walk and love Him as the Catholic Church does their job of reviewing the books.

Every day as I walk with Jesus and let God love me through Jesus, He sees my faith and love grow to a deeper level. The more I breathe with Him and trust in Him, the stronger I will become. I will be one with God.

I am keeping faith in the Lord and He knows I will succeed in all that He asks of me. It does not matter how long it takes for His books to open the doors of the Catholic Church.

*I will continue to dream, meditate, pray, and love God/Jesus daily. That is the least I can do for Him, for He is always loving me and finding me worthy of walking as one with Him. He has given me a second chance at love and life with God, the Father.*

*

I will now research Yasser Arafat. My knowledge and understanding of this man is next to nothing. He is a man that God has brought forward before. I feel in my heart the connection between "the God of Yasser Arafat," "Trump," and "The razorback wolf." They are a sign of trouble that is brewing and causing God's anger around the world.

God sees all, and God knows all. He will not let those who are in charge continue to spin His world out of control.

**"I've got this."** I heard these words from the Father a few times today, as He asked me to breathe and just love Him.

# THESE FLAMES OF LOVE

*Her heart beats to my own and the flames grow with every beat*

4:40 p.m.
October 21, 2017

> **Word of the day: Humility-** The Bible describes humility as meekness, lowliness and absence of self. The Greek word translated "humility" in Colossians 3:12 and elsewhere literally means "lowliness of mind," so we see that humility is a heart attitude, not merely an outward demeanor. One may put on an outward show of humility but still have a heart full of pride and arrogance. Jesus said that those who are "poor in spirit" would have the kingdom of heaven. Being poor in spirit means that only those who admit to an absolute bankruptcy of spiritual worth will inherit eternal life. Therefore, humility is a prerequisite for the Christian.

As I walk with Jesus daily and feel the love that God holds for me through Jesus, I am taught lessons - lessons in love and lessons in faith.

God taught me the love He has held for me all my life. This is the very reason He chose me for the *Second Coming of the Christ Child*.

I feel Jesus Christ living within my body. My consciousness is one with the Father's and I only ask daily now for strength to hold tight as God's plans and wishes come true. I have tried all my life to love and be-loved. God assures me I have not failed Him in that area at all, ever.

God teaches me the word *humility* today and it is a lesson in my heart that I sometimes struggle with. Not letting other people's opinions effect my heart or the way I speak or feel. I stay quiet and let them have their say and voice their opinions. As I walk daily with Jesus, I am learning copious amounts of *grace*. I will research this word now, for I feel this word in my heart as God holds my hands to help me hold my tongue, to help me be humble, and to help me learn from others.

**Grace-** (in Christian belief) the free and unmerited favor of God, as manifested in the salvation of sinners and the bestowal of blessing. A. Unmerited divine assistance given humans for their regeneration or sanctification B. a virtue coming from God.

# GOD'S WORLD

## *God's Quest for Salvation*

7:17 pm
October 22, 2017

The phrase **"Quest for Salvation"** is something Jesus and I have researched before.

I am God's own chosen bride for the *end days*. I trust in all that God gives me. The books that we write together are a gift to the Catholic Church: Monumental visions and dreams the Father brings forward for my own learning. He asks me to continue to share these lessons with the Elders of the Catholic Church.

Jesus' own Temple is that of all the Churches. His first Temple, however, consists of the bodies of our children. God lives within each one of us. His heart beats within each one of us. We are the mystical body of Christ.[42]

As I walk daily with Jesus Christ, He communicates copious amounts of information. None are as important as this fact: *God's very heart is fading fast.* Jesus assures me that **God** will go on - God cannot perish.

*"Our children are running in fear". "Too many of our children are running with the devil".*

Lessons to me from the Father: *I have lived this fear of the devil, and I have run from God a good portion of my life. At the same time, I always kept God up front and within my heart. (People are contradictory!)*

God tells me my heart is the purest of hearts. I am a strong, passionate and loving woman. A woman He created for the very trying times our children are facing.

---

[42] source in Paul

I am often given manifestations of the body and today has been very painful. I feel the pains of the Father, Son, and the Mother of God.

I wake early this morning and we prepare for our day. My lungs are very heavy. I have difficulty breathing. As I go through the day, my throat pains me.

Jesus asks me, *"Why, do your lungs and throat hurt, my love?"*

Before the question is fully out of my "heart" (where all my communication starts), I tell Jesus they hurt because of the chemical warfare that is coming.

*"Very good. You rarely miss a lesson. It is close now, and I need you to be strong."*

I have received visions of epic proportions for the past two years. These painful images come when I am still - as I sit in a chair, lie in a bed, or rest in a tub of water.

These are dreams with meanings that God brings forward, and He asks me to share all that He has given to me; to share with those who can help the mystical heart and body of Christ in these times of testing.

Two days ago, I felt sand in my eyes. I am asked to record its meaning here. This message has been brought forward before in our teachings.

Words from the Father: *"The sand will fly." "The dust will fly." "The clouds will open up."*

*All hell has been breaking loose for a while now. God shows His righteous anger through the natural disasters that are occurring around the world. He has been sending me warnings of these events for over eleven years. I, however, was not prepared or ready for the level of communication that Jesus needed from me back in 2006.*

God has plans and He tells me, ***"The perfect storm has been created in this world."***

I know and understand most of what God shows me. Where He wants it to go is evident to me. Our children's lives are at stake and His heart is disappearing fast.

***"Our little angels are flying to the heavens and to Purgatory in large numbers."***

Today God reminds me of the drawings that the angels have helped me put to paper: I have drawn the *Titanic*.

God's very Heart is "at the bottom of the Ocean," and the ocean is a representation of God's tears.

*"God's Church is at the bottom of the ocean."* This leads me to tonight's entry into God's books of Revelations.

I thought we would write about President Trump and World War III that is already here. The threats are in the news bulletin today: *North Korea accuses US of declaring war -Washington (CNN) North Korea's Foreign Minister Ri Yong Ho on Monday accused US President Donald Trump of declaring war on his country by tweeting over the weekend that North Korea "won't be around much longer". "Last weekend Trump claimed our leadership wouldn't be around and declared a war on our country." Ri said, according to an official translation of his remarks to reporters in New York.* [43]

I see Jesus as He stands before me today. His head is hung low and God tells me, ***"I am ashamed of those in charge."***

I have seen this vision of Jesus before. In my second book, *Love Letters in the Sand,* I write about this shame that He is now showing me he feels again.

---

43

God is on His knees daily. Jesus Christ kneels in front of me almost daily begging for *Mercy* from our children, begging them to open their hearts and to stop this madness.

I cry tears with the Creator of the world. He reminds that me I am the Mother of God, that I am standing in place in the present day for Mother Mary. I feel Mother Mary's ovarian pains. I feel pains in my breasts and I feel the arrows within my heart.

I feel the pains of Jesus Christ.

Manifestations of the body have been numerous over the past two years.

None are as painful or scary as the *chemical burns* that God allows me to feel as I sit in a tub of water. This is painful and scary. Jesus tells me, **"It is coming."**

*

## Back to God's Quest for Salvation

As I write and research, God guides me to a subject that He and I have talked about before. We, however, have not written on this subject and He asks me to open another can of worms. It includes those who stand in His place in Jesus' own Temple, the Catholic Church.

*News bulletin: Conservative Roman Catholic theologians accuse Pope of spreading heresy*

*Several dozen tradition-minded Roman Catholic theologians, priests and academics have formally accused Pope Francis of spreading heresy with his 2016 opening to divorced and civilly remarried Catholics.*

*In a 25-page letter delivered to Francis last month and provided Saturday to The Associated Press, the 62 signatories issued a "filial correction" to the pope—a measure they said hadn't been employed since the 14th century.*

*The letter accused Francis of propagating seven heretical positions concerning marriage, moral life and the sacraments with his 2016 document "The Joy of Love" and subsequent "acts, words and omissions."*

*None of the signatories of the newsletter is a cardinal, and the highest-ranking churchman listed is actually someone whose organization has no legal standing in the Catholic Church; Bishop B., superior of the break way Society of St. Pius X. Several other signatories are well-known admirers of the old Latin Mass which Bishop B. followers celebrate.*

*But organizers said the initiative was nevertheless significant and a sign of the concern among a certain contingent of academic and pastors over Francis' positions, which they said posed a danger to the faithful.*

*"There is a role for theologians and philosophers to explain to people the church's teaching, to correct misunderstandings," said Joseph Shaw, a spokesman for the initiative, signatory of the correction and senior research fellow in moral in philosophy at Oxford University.*

*When it was released in April of 2016, "the Joy of Love" immediately sparked controversy because it opened the door to letting civilly remarried Catholics receive Communion. Church teachings holds, that unless these Catholics obtain an annulment—a church decree that their first marriage was invalid-they cannot receive the sacraments, since they are seen as committing adultery.*

*Francis didn't create a church-wide pass for these Catholics but suggested-in vague terms and strategically placed footnotes-that Bishops and priests could do so on a case-by-case basis after accompanying them on a spiritual journey of discernment. Subsequent comments and writings have made clear the intended wiggle room, part of his belief that God's mercy extends in particular to sinners and that the Eucharist isn't a prize for the perfect but nourishment for the weak. Shaw said none of the four cardinals involved in the initial "dubbia" letter, nor any other cardinal, was involved in the "filial correction."*

*Organizers said the last time such a correction was issued was to Pope John XXII in 1333 for errors which he later recanted.*[44]

> *Pope Francis offers hope to divorced Catholics, says no to gay marriage.*[45]

Pope Francis stands in place of God. He is the "One" closest to God. He is the one chosen to head the Catholic Church, with Jesus' direction.

There are so many issues and so much turmoil surrounding the lost children of the world! Times have changed; it is time for the Church to stop the fear and judgement.

***"Holding God's own children at arm's length."*** This is a term Jesus and God have used before in my writings. He walks back and forth in front of me. Jesus' anger and frustration at the Church shows as I write the last few paragraphs in this entry.

**"Jesus Christ, Our Son died on the cross for the sins of the children of the world".**

The passion of the Christ is something I have never experienced so completely "first hand" as when I sit in meditation or love God as a true wife. Reliving those final moments of Our Son who suffered greatly on the cross over two-thousand years ago. The arrows strike my own Immaculate Heart very hard today. Arrows of my own and God reminds me today that I am "The Mother of God". Chosen before the beginning of time, to help resurrect the lost lambs of the world. Bringing Salvation back to help raise the spirits from the dead in Our children who continue to run from God's Own True Love and Light!

---

[44] Cited from: Catholics News.com

[45]

# "The Passion of Christ"

Photo By: Shutterstock

God has brought me a vision over and over during the past few months. As Jesus walks with me daily, He reminds me of His sacrifice on the cross. His life was given up for the sins of God's children, His own children.

*"Do this in memory of me."*

*"Bring my lost lambs to the Temple and give them bread and wine. Let them eat, and drink of the cup of knowledge."* These are God's very words. The Eucharist is God's very body and the wine is His blood, shed for us to help those in need of strength to get through life's trials.

The Passion of God enters through my fingers and I feel my heart and it pains me severely as I write this passage.

Tears lie close to the surface, and they belong to the Father, Son and Mother Mary.

A lesson for me: *God tells me I am worthy of receiving the strength of the Eucharist. I need His body and blood. I need His strength within me. I am a sinner and God loves me very much. A chosen bride in His time of greatest need.*

I left a failed marriage to save my own sanity. I have not yet had this marriage annulled, yet God speaks through me at the same time that my godmother begs me "not to receive" the Eucharist. She believes my sins outweigh my "worthiness" of receiving this very special rite of Christ.

As God lives within my body, He steps forward and I tell her through the Passion of Christ, "***God says I am worthy.***"

God tells me, "***you have gone too long without my love.***" Jesus Christs' anger and frustration came forward over 3 months ago when I went to receive the Eucharist. God stepped forward within me, giving me the ability to stand up to an amazingly faithful woman who loves God like no other woman I have known. Yet, the passion within me, (was that of Jesus Christ) and I knew it was not me saying these words.

I ask again, who determined after Christ died on the cross for our sins an individual unworthy to receive Jesus' strength and love through His body and blood?

It is a hard lesson for me to come forward and write, for my own humanness gets in the way. God's words flow through my fingers and I feel the love He holds for me. I feel this through the hunger in my "solar plexus" (my stomach- God's hunger for our love) and the "root chakra" (the kisses that God/Jesus pour down upon me as He lives, breathes and loves me through my own body).

\*

A connection to me. Another heart to be added to this special jar of hearts that God asks me to take on as my own. Saint Faustina is another special woman in history. My own love story of Jesus is similar to St. Faustina's. God tells me my consciousness is His own. I have breathed Him into life through my own heart, mind, and body. The journey that the Master Teacher Himself has lead me down.

# WHO IS JESUS CHRIST?

### *Jesus Christ is the love of my life...*

At 4:30 a.m.
October 25, 2017

I wake as I feel warmth beside me. I see Mother Mary and she stands beside the bed. She tells me, *"I have always been with you, since birth. I came in with you and I will go out with you."*

I fall asleep on and off as usual and I feel Mother Mary's presence beside me. I see her white robe and blue cloak. She is facing away from me in the early hours of the morning. I am given the meaning of Mother Mary facing away from me. *"You are following in my footsteps."*

In and out of sleep in the night, I feel Jesus and He puts His arms around me. He lies with me and we converse as I close my eyes. God and Jesus hold me throughout the night. As I dream and sleep lightly, I hear them talking and I am not aware of all that is said. I just know they are there.

I write this morning and God/Jesus love and hold me tight. I feel ecstasy within my body. I am asked by Mother Mary and Jesus to take time out for myself. I call in sick. I still feel the heaviness within my lungs and my throat is on fire. God is waiting for the battle to begin: *the chemical warfare.*

Jesus asks me to love Him today. ***"Choose me over the money."*** I tell Him, *"I do choose you, my Lord. Today, tomorrow and throughout all eternity, I choose to walk as one with you over and over again. You are my own love and my own light throughout all time and space."*

As a special gift to me God guides me to another amazing book. He asks me to add this passage from this book. It has His approval, for if not He would not ask me to add it to His own books of Revelations.

***"Only God can forgive."***

***"Are your sins forgiven?"***

*Jesus came into this world to provide the means of forgiveness for the sins of all mankind. Has that purpose been fulfilled for you? Have your sins been forgiven, wiped clean? That all depends on whether you have called upon Him for His forgiveness. If you have not (or are not sure you have), I urge you today.*

*He has paid the eternal debt of your sin on the cross, only three things remain for you to do:*

*1. admit it was for you and your sins that Jesus died.*

*2. Believe He has risen from the dead.*

*3. Call upon Him to forgive you and save your soul.*

*If you do those three things, Jesus assures you that you will be with Him in eternity, just as the thief on the cross is now with Him. But following through on these three things does more than gain forgiveness of sins and assures you of a place in heaven. It will empower you, to follow Jesus' example of granting forgiveness to those who wronged against you. This is one of the greatest wonders of salvation.* [46]

*

---

46

Words given to me from the Father and Jesus Christ as I wake this morning:

**"*The Book of Saint Matthew.*"**

I find this and skim it with my eyes. God/Jesus share with me what they want highlighted for the lesson of the day:

**The Gospel According to St. Matthew**
*The writer of the first Gospel, as all agree, was Matthew, called also Levi, a Jew of Galilee who had taken service as a tax-gatherer under the Roman oppressor. He was, therefore one of the hated and ill-reputed publicans. Theme: the scope and purpose of the books are indicated in the first verse. Matthew is the "book" of the generation of Jesus Christ, the son of David, the Son of Abraham". This connects Him at once with two of the most important of the Old Testament covenants: The Davidic Covenant of kingship, and the and the Abrahamic Covenant of promise.*[47]

**God/Jesus highlight these words:**

Promise

Twofold Character

Obedient unto death

Genealogy

Rejection

Great Glory

Sacrificial death of the Son

---

[47]

Manifestation

King of the Jews

The official genealogy and birth of the King

The Kingdom at hand

The mysteries of the Kingdom

The Risen Lord

I never quite know where God is leading me until I stop and reread and listen to my heart. As I type the lesson I am given, immediately the connection associated with this lesson.

God asked me to be His wife nearly two years ago. He asks me daily on His knees to marry Him. He tells me, ***"I will continue to do this daily until it [this work] is accepted by the Catholic Church."***

I have already accepted this position of honor. God brought me back from the dead for this journey. I accept all He gives me.

*

God has asked me to "adopt" all the children of the world as my own; to love and teach them and to help them see the love that He has for each one of them. He has long asked me to take on the role of Mother Mary. He continually calls me *Mother Mary* in our most intimate moments.

I tell Him daily, "I will do my best."

So, as I reread and write about the "Book of Saint Matthew," I get the connection.

He wants me to take on the name and identity of The Mother of God - Mother Mary.

I have already received Mother Mary's blessings. I received a large bouquet of red roses. I received a beautiful set of Rosary beads of my own, from Mother Mary.

I have received acceptance and love from Mother Mary regarding my relationship with Jesus Christ.

I know not everyone will understand this journey I find myself on with God. He, however, has directed me to the Catholic Church for a specific reason. This is the church that He founded.[48] I know and understand the reasoning behind it. I ask God daily, on bended knee with tears flowing, to please open the doors so I can help bring our children the Mercy they deserve.

I understand the trying times we are all faced with. I understand the fear and hatred and unforgiveness that our children carry. I understand the abuses and the mental imbalances our children are experiencing. I have lived it!

Writing books of epic proportions for God has not been an easy task to undertake, and He reminds me today of how proud He is of my devotion and the love that I have shown to Him and to Jesus. He understands the fear that I keep in my heart, for He knows the visions, dreams and meditations that He brings forward are not easy. These are the Lessons that I accept as my new soul-path.

I try to help the Father in His deepest darkest hours as He contemplates the ruin of our children's lives.

God shares with me a great deal. Many will not be comfortable with all the subjects we touch on. He also encourages me just to love and trust in Him. I do that with all my might.

*

---

[48] At Pentecost, when HE SENT THE HOLY SPIRIT UPON THE APOSTLES IN TONGUES OF FIRE. THIS IS CONSIDERED THE BIRTH DAY OF THE CHURCH.

As I write books for the love I hold for Jesus Christ, He shares with me that no one knows Him better than I do. I have an intimate relationship with the Father and the Son as we walk, talk, sing, and love at all hours of the day and night.

Many tears have fallen from my eyes again today. None are as painful to me as the tears I cry for the Father, for the children of the world.

Jesus Christ is the face of God, brought down to the earth planes through the Holy Spirit; Mother Mary and Jesus Christ have always been with me.

# HIS ADORATION

*"Ask and it will be given to you; search, and you will find; knock, and the door will be opened for you."*
*Jesus Christ*[49]

8:11 p.m.
November 1, 2017

I have tried with all my might to follow the directions that I hear from my own heart.

The love that is poured down from the Heavens is so overpowering. I feel His adoration today as we make love.

I am not feeling well at all today and my throat is on fire. I rest most of the day. I do, however, take time to make it to Mass this morning and I feel so much closer to God when I can be in His presence in the church.

His love flows freely today, and I sit among the children. There are so many of them today at St. Mary's Catholic Church. I take the sight of them all in, young and old alike. God has asked me to take all His children and adopt them as my own. I accept this great honor.

I only wonder what, where, when and how this will occur?

God feels my illness today and He takes it easy on me as I sit in the chair at Mass. He steps back and just lets me observe all that He wants me to see.

Jesus keeps my heart light. He feels the tears and the sickness in my lungs and throat. A manifestation this morning, and I get proof of this later in the day.

---

[49] Biblical source

119

Jesus and I go home, and we rest, and I go straight to bed. My heart is heavy with the visions in the night and messages of the chemical warfare that God continually brings forward. Jesus tells me, ***"It won't be long now."***

I ask where and when, but He won't allow me to know the details. He has given me enough. This has been coming for a long time. God shares with me that this is His war. He tells me, ***"You have done your part. I need you to rest and love Me."***

We struggle today to love one another and get past the visions and knowing of the chemical warfare that is coming. He begs me to love Him.

I break down and cry several times and He tries to hold me. I give in. He knows my heart is very heavy. No word still from the Catholic Church or Monsignor 'D'. No counsel from the material world; and some days I don't know how much more I can take. God assures me He won't let me fall. He tells me I am my mother's daughter and I am stronger than anyone knows.

We cover with the sheets for I feel I have a fever today. My body is overheated; it is the love of Jesus and God within that causes this heat today. Their love for me is overpowering.

As we connect on a personal level I am shown the hand of God reaching down to Adam again.

He tells me ***"I love you like I have no other woman. You hold me so tight, I can't breathe."***

God makes love to me and I feel a very painful "clamping" of sorts on the top of my head. As this pain comes in while we make love, God shows me the *Adoration of the Eucharist* and it is placed on my head as a crown.

The crown with the points of the 12 stars is what I thought God had placed on my head. He tells me, *"No."* He gives me the words, ***"You are the living host of God."***

I am then given the words, ***"Adoration of the Eucharist."***

We hold one another and fall asleep for a bit. I feel Jesus holding me and I know Jesus and God are one. We will walk, talk, sing, and love one another until I take my last breath.

I feel the negative energies come and go today. It is something I am getting used to. God tests me daily and asks me to recognize these as tests. I don't like to fight with Him and He knows it breaks my heart when He brings in the negative to help me come back to His own loving arms.

He is the Creator of all good and evil and I am tested with my own understanding and the understanding of our children, the "lost souls" of the world. Those who don't have God close to their own hearts. Those who run in fear and create a world filled with chaos.

I am reminded today as I walk with Jesus of more of the messages that lead me up to this "ill" feeling within today.

I feel tonight like a sledge-hammer is coming down on the top of my head. It is very painful, and I don't need to ask too many questions, for the visions and information that Jesus shares with me today make it all come together.

*

### Satan

Does he exist?

*News bulletin today: Russian 'Cannibal Couple' suspected of killing and eating up to 30 people. Authorities were said to have found pickled human remains in glass jars and pots of severed parts in the*

***couple's home…drugged, skinned alive and then killed. Then eating them alive.*** [50]

Not a pretty headline or a pretty sight for the investigators who stumbled upon this horrific crime.

God shows me the dark side of our children. I see reality at its worst and He tells me I am very naïve when it comes to some of the people in the material world.

I have lived traumas and dramas and still I believe the devil does not exist. This news bulletin is proof of the horrors that God endures.

Mental Illness, Healthcare Crisis, Political Arena out of control, Threats of World War III, Isis, Natural Disasters, Homeless and starving children around the world, Religious upheaval with child molestation allegations, Elder Abuse, Child Abuse, Animal Abuse, it goes on and on.

Our children are out of control. God's own heart center is on the line. God tells me He is often breathless through the choices of our children.

He feels this breathlessness through the energy field of the world. He feels it through the bodies of our children.

"The Walking Dead" is reality for so many of them.

This is the very reason why I feel the sledge hammer on my head today. God is reminding me I feel His pain through my body. I feel the pain of our children through the lessons that He brings forward for me to teach and share with the Catholic Church.

I still wonder tonight as I hold His hand and just journal and love Him through the typewritten word, *how do I get where you need me to be?*

\*

# Bible lesson of the day: Psalm 143

## *Psalm 143*

### *A Psalm of David*

*Hear my prayer, O Lord, give ear to my supplications: in thy faithfulness answer me, and in thy righteousness. 2) and enter not into judgement with thy servant; for in thy sight shall no man living be justified. 3) For the enemy hath persecuted my soul, he hath smitten my life down to the ground he hath made me to dwell in darkness, as those that have been long dead. 4) Therefore, is my spirit overwhelmed within me; my heart within me is desolate. 5) I remember the days of old; I meditate on all thy works' I must on the work of thy hands. 6) I stretch forth my hands unto thee; my soul thirsteth after thee, as a thirsty land Selah. 7) Hear me speedily: O Lord: my spirit faileth hide not thy face from me, lest I be like unto them that go down into the pit. 8) Cause me to hear thy loving kindness in the morning; for in thee do I trust; cause me to know the way wherein I should walk, for I lift up my soul unto thee. 9) Deliver me, O Lord, from mine enemies; I flee unto thee to hide me. 10) Teach me to do thy will, for thou art my God: thy spirit is good; lead me into the land of uprightness. 11) Quicken me, O Lord, for thy name's sake: for thy righteousness, sake bring my soul out of trouble. 12) And of thy mercy cut off mine enemies and destroy all them that afflict my soul; for I am thy servant.*[51]

Messages of God's love for our children: God reaches out to me through Jesus Christ. He tells me I am *The Incarnate Word*. I am *The Holy Grail* of today. I am God's own wife and Jesus' own bride. A message from King David today - I am asked to record this verse from the Bible, Psalm 143.

God is each one of us. He has taught me the Trinity and I believe all that He gives me. We are His eyes and ears, and many do not know this. So many Lessons today, and I can never record them all, for they come in

---

[51] Cited from: CatholicGO.org

like waves. Tears of love flow today, and God is so very proud of the books I have written for Him. Jesus holds me tight today and I love Him so very much. The Father and Son stand tall today and salute me for they say, ***"You are Our hero."***

**Invocation for today: Prayers to Jesus and Mary for Mercy**

**Lord Jesus Christ, eternal and Merciful God, Creator
and Redeemer of all, listen to my prayer.
For the love Thou doth bear to those who ask forgiveness,
Look on me with mercy, as once Thou
didst look on Mary Magdalene,
And on Peter who denied Thee
Look on me, Lord Jesus Christ, as Thou
didst look on Thy Mother, Mary,
Standing in sorrow beneath thy Cross.
Let me feel in my heart her compassion for Thee,
and let my eyes weep for Thy sorrows,
Caused by my sinful life.
Call me back from the darkness to my Father's house,
Give me a new heart
And a place at Thy side in the banquet Thou hast prepared for me.
Amen**

**Hail Mary, my joy, my glory, my heart and my soul!
Thou art all mine through thy mercy, and I am all
thine. But I am not thine completely enough.
Destroy in me all that may be displeasing to God. Place
and cultivate in me everything that is pleasing to thee.
Amen**[52]

\*

---

[52] Cited from: CatholicGO.org

# THE STARS FALL FROM THE SKY

9:34 p.m.
November 2, 201753

---

**Word of the day: Smite[53]**

**Smite-** "Transitive verb". 1) To strike sharply or heavily especially with the hand or an implement held in the hand. 2) a: To kill or severely injure; smiting. B: To attack or inflict suddenly and injuriously. Smitten by disease.

What is the meaning of "smote" in the Bible?

"Sense of slay in combat" (c.1300) is from Biblical expression smite to death, first attested c. 1200 meaning "visit disastrously" is mid-12 c. also Biblical meaning. Meaning "strike with passion or emotion" is from c. 1300."

**History lesson of the day: Saint Peregrine[54]**

Saint Peregrine Laziosi (Pellegrino Latiosi) (c. 1260-1 May 1345) is an Italian saint of the Servite Order (friar Order Servants of Mary). He is the patron saint for persons suffering from cancer, aids, or other illness'.

Born: c. 1260, Forli, Italy

Died: May 1, 1345

Canonized: December 27, 1726, by Pope Benedict XIII

Attributes: one leg covered in cancerous sore, a staff

Patronage: persons suffering from cancer, aids, or other illnesses.

---

*

---

[53] Saint Peregrine research: http://wikipedia.org
54

**Plagues and sickness keep growing as time goes on.**

Many messages come to me throughout the day. I have a constant connection to the Creator of the world through the love I hold for Jesus Christ. History lessons are brought forward to help me understand the importance of the journey God finds me worthy of. Walking as one with the Father, Son and the Holy Spirit.

Since I am fully awakened to the love God holds for me and all our children, He wakes me through my consciousness. I feel God wake me through my brain vibrating.

I smile and say, "Good morning." Never a more loving man could I have encountered in my entire existence! Jesus Christ's birth, through Mother Mary was a miracle; God shares with me that my own resurrection is His greatest miracle of today. I have come to accept it as my own truth.

My soul-purpose and path were pre-destined, and who am I to question God?

Many Angels and Saints have graced me with their appearance for over two years now. By the Grace of God is how all of this has happened. Jesus Christ has been giving me all the lessons brought forward; He has been teaching me the truth of God's love and mysteries. These are not always easy lessons and He is so very proud of me for accepting all His love through these lessons.

Early this morning I drive home from working another 18- hour shift, and I am not as tired as some would expect. This is a miracle in itself; God holds me up daily through the Angels and Saints present within my body. I experience the *'life force of God'*.

I come home from church and I am given the name Saint Peregrine and I am then given the knowledge that my cousin Cherice is with me. I have been able to recognize and understand the Angels present and those passed who step forward to help me. This happens through God's grace and the energy field that surrounds me; blessings from the Father through Jesus Christ.

Cherice was a loving and devoted mother of two beautiful babies. Her life was cut short and it was by the dis-ease of cancer, a well-known killer within my family. Cancer has taken the lives of many of those that I have held close to my own heart.

Over the past few days, I have been asked to please start praying more and writing less, which is a hard thing for me to do. I have come to crave writing about the love that God holds for all our children. I want to preserve the love that God has for all of us through the visions and love that He showers me with daily. I want to help all people understand the Creator of the world and to show just how passionate and loving Jesus Christ is.

Magic and mysteries. Faith and hope. Love and Glory. All come together for me when I think of the Creator of the world. These few words sum up my personal knowledge of God.

Not all will understand the intimate relationship that I have with the Father.[55] Not all will love the messages, visions or truths that the Father shares with me.

God shares with me so many beautiful things. He tells me no one could have done what I have done, for it was my destiny to be His own wife.

As I learn of Saint Peregrine, I learn that He did great works for God, keeping faith and love within his own heart and forging on.

I am asked to hold tight to Jesus' arm and walk on proud as we wait for God's books to work their magic through the Catholic Church. I struggle with this some days and God knows the reasons behind this.

---

[55] blessed are those not scandalized by me.

It's not that I don't trust Him. It's not that I don't love Him. It's that I know through my own experiences and the lives that I am in contact with daily that God's heart is truly in jeopardy. Fading every day.

It's very painful to see the visions that God shares with me. To know God is on His knees daily begging our children for mercy. God is begging them to open their hearts and to love themselves. Begging them to love their own brethren. This is heart wrenching and very painful. To know I can't do anything other than record His tears and the pain He allows me to feel through my own body. This *knowing* He shares with me daily in private as I walk in the wilderness among the lost souls of our children.

## TEAR DROPS ON MY PILLOW

### *His arms surround me; and I fight Him tonight*

*I want to be alone and Jesus won't allow it*
*The tears that I cry are for the children of the world*
*Sad, lonely, sick, scared, hurting, abused, and dying...*
*So much pain comes to me*
*I close my eyes*
*Tears on my pillow and Jesus stands at the door and I see Him*
*He waits*
*naked*
*Waits for me to ask Him to love me and I can't*
*My heart breaking*
*He feels it*
*Visions flood my senses*
*I will drown in*
*The sorrows of our children*
*Visions and dreams*
*Mine by the grace of God*
*My senses sinking*
*My children suffering*

*God shows me a*
*Snow globe*
*I see the stable*
*I see the manger and Baby Jesus*
*I see Mother Mary and Joseph*
*I am, swimming inside it*
*At the bottom a book*
*Pages oozing His Precious Blood*

\*

# GOD'S CHRISTMAS TRUCE

## *O' Holy Night the Stars are brightly shining* [56]

10:24 p.m.
November 4, 2017

Another tearful day spent loving Jesus Christ. This is a journey I wouldn't change for all the gold in the world. We walk as one and I am grateful today once more, for God loving me this much. He sustains me daily and shares with me the love He holds for our children.

So much devastation is going on in the material world. Jesus continually begs me to hold tight to His arm today. Reality sinks in as so much chaos continues in the world. I try with all my might to let God handle all that is going on with our children.

I ask Him, how do I give the lives and hearts of our children to you and allow you to take care of the issues at hand, if you continually bring devastation and destruction to me in visions and dreams?

Looking through the eyes of God, I have seen history from days gone by. God brought forward nearly two years ago the death, destruction and the demise of humanity. It was a horrific sight and I felt the pains of it in my heart and my body.

With no one to counsel me, I hold tight to Jesus tonight even though He shows me His naked body in the doorway.

Jesus Christ lives within my body and He holds me tight from the inside out.

I hear Him tonight and He begs me, ***"Please, breathe with me. You are breaking my heart."***

---

[56]

Jesus tries to console me, and it takes a while for me to work through this deep sadness in my heart. My heart feels Mother Mary's arrows and they are stronger than usual tonight.

I hear of the death of another large group of our children gathered at another concert. So much death and so many lives affected by this one incident!

The children reach out to me as they try to find their way to heaven. These lost souls are searching for the higher planes. Some of these precious babies try desperately to get to heaven. God brings them in. I don't get names today, just their faces as they reach out to me, as if I can help them get where they need to be. I'm not supposed to feel this sadness. I am supposed to let God take it from me.

Jesus told me two days ago as He stepped forward with Mother Teresa, *"Now is the time for prayer."* With these words from Jesus and Mother Teresa, I bend down today and pray for all our children. I pray for the lost souls searching for heaven above and those running from God's love and light on the earth plane.

Today Jesus tries to raise my spirits. We prepare for Christmas. He has been giving me the phrase *Christmas Truce* for about a year and a half now. He has sung, "Santa Claus is coming to town" for two years. I hold tight to so many of His promises, for the lives of our children are at stake. The future of our children is hanging in the balance. I hope for Peace and Love above all.

I give these all back to Him: the projects and plans that God has asked me to take on as my own. For I still wonder, how do I get these to the point of "fruition" without help?

No doors are opening from the Catholic Church. More tears fall from my eyes tonight as I try to catch my breath. I beg Jesus for mercy for our children. I ask for counsel and I have faith that God can make this happen.

I have called the Diocese twice to speak to Monsignor 'D'. I have received no call back. No word of encouragement that the books have even been opened. Sadness takes over and God knows me better than anyone. He knows I will never give up. He knows my feet will hit the ground running tomorrow. I will still love Him. I will still work magic and put a smile on my face. I will fake it for I have learned from the Master Teacher Himself how to walk in Grace…

\*

# THE GRACE OF AN ANGEL

*Her smile fades in and out as I teach her*
*Lessons in history*
*The past meshes with her present*
*And we both hold hope for the future*
*The grace and beauty of her - I see it grow stronger every day*
*Mother Mary is my own true love*
*My own true light*
*As her love for me grows stronger every day I see*
*The Mother of God emerge through*
*The grace in her own Immaculate Heart*
*One in the Holy Spirit*
*Father, Son and the Mother of God*

# GLORY BE

### *The Most Holy Virgin*
*Who never lets herself be out done in love and liberty, seeing that we give ourselves entirely to her... meets us in the same spirit. She also gives her whole self, and gives it in an unspeakable manner, to him who gives all to her. She causes him to be engulfed in the abyss of her graces. She adorns him with her merits; she supports him with her power; she illuminates him with her light; she enflames him with her love; she communicates to him her virtues; her humility, her faith, her purity, and the rest. In a word, as that consecrated person is all Mary's, so Mary is all his.* [57]

4:19 p.m.
November 5, 2017

I have been working through many emotions over the past few weeks. In letting God take over, I have struggled to put words to paper for the Father, Son, and Mother Mary.

Learning to sit in grace is not easy. It is not easy to have the patience of a Saint when you see the visions that God shares with me daily.

Mother Mary holds my heart today and it beats within the walls of my chest.

Jesus' Sacred Heart covers my own heart and both the Mother and Father's deep passionate love have swallowed me up.

I am led to another book and it is all to help me understand the love I hold for Mother Mary and Jesus. Nothing is as important as learning of this deep love I hold for the Father and the Creator of the world.

**Book of the week:** *33 Days to Morning Glory: A Do-it-yourself Retreat in Preparation for Marian Consecration.* [58]

---

[57] *Glory Be Cited from:* CatholicGo.org
[58]

Another gift from God and I am grateful for all the special people in my life. A strong woman of Catholic faith purchased this book and knows in her heart that it was meant for me. I thank you for all the gifts given to me, my Lord.

God has me understand over the past few days that He is trying, through the books that we write together, to prove the miracle He performed through my own death and resurrection. He breathed into me His breath of life, and I believe His power, and, more importantly, I believe His deep love for me.

God/Jesus have shared so much love with me I can hardly contain it all within my heart. To bring a lost lamb such as myself back to life after I wished so many times to end it is a great miracle.

I am grateful for a second chance at life and I am overawed by the love poured down upon me from the heavens above. So many Angels and Saints have graced me with their presence. It is all by the power of God! The full Graces of God are upon me. I bow to the Father and the Son for the deep love they show to me daily.

A reading from the book God places in front of me for my own understanding of how He wants me to accept the alteration of my soul to become one with Mother Mary. He wishes me to purify my heart and soul. He will lead me down a path of righteousness, so that I can help those living in a hell of their own to understand God's deep love and devotion to the Mother of God and all our children.

## GIVING MYSELF, FULLY TO GOD THROUGH JESUS AND MOTHER MARY

**Word of the day: Consecration-**To make holy or to dedicate to a higher purpose.

Consecrated life- "In the canon law of the Catholic Church, is a stable form of Christian living by those faithful who are called to follow Jesus Christ in a more exacting way recognized by the church".

Consecrated Women- "Are a branch of the regnum Christi movement made up of lay women who dedicate themselves full-time to apostolate". "They live consecrated life in the church within the lay state".

Consecrating yourself to God- "Dedicating your heart to God". "To consecrate yourself is to answer God's call to spiritual Consecration". "This means making conscious, willing decision to dedicate your soul, mind, heart and body to God".

**What does the Bible say about Consecration?** In the Bible the word consecration means "the separation of oneself from things that are unclean, especially anything that would contaminate one's relationship with a perfect God". Consecration also carries the connotations of sanctification, holiness, or purity.

The importance of being consecrated or pure in our relationship with god is emphasized in an incident in the book of Joshua. After forty years in the wilderness, the children of Israel were about to cross over the Jordan River into the Promised Land. They were then given a command and a promise: "Joshua told the people, 'Consecrate yourselves, for tomorrow the Lord will do amazing things among you." (Joshua 3:5).

**How do I consecrate myself to God?** Dedicate your heart to God. To consecrate yourself is to answer God's call to spiritual consecration.

Reflect on your motives, repent, be baptized, separate yourself from the evils of the world, draw closer to God, and stay committed. [59]

*"Saint Julie Ann's name is written on Our Hearts"*

Mary leads us to Jesus and doesn't take away our crosses. In fact, those who are particularly beloved by Mary often have more crosses than others, but Mary makes the crosses sweet and light:

[59] Consecration to Mary and Jesus Cited from 33 Days to Morning Glory

It is quite true that the most faithful servants of the Blessed Virgin, being also her greatest favorites, receive from her the greatest graces and favors from Heaven, which are crosses. But I maintain that it is also the servants of Mary who carry these crosses with more ease, more merit, and more glory. That which would stay the progress of another thousand times over, or perhaps would make him fall, does not stop their steps, but rather enables them to advance; because that good Mother, all full of grace and of the unction of the Holy Spirit, prepares her servants' crosses with so much maternal sweetness and pure love as to make them gladly acceptable, no matter how bitter they may be in themselves; it's just as a person would not be able to eat unripe fruits without a great effort which he could hardly keep up, unless they had been preserved in sugar.

We make more progress in a brief period of submission to and dependence on Mary than in whole years of following our own will and relying upon ourselves.

By this practice, faithfully observed, you will give Jesus more glory in a month than by any other practice, however difficult, in many years.

**{True devotees of Mary} have such a facility in carrying the yoke of Jesus Christ that they feel almost nothing of its weight.**

Mary puts herself around {her true children} and accompanies them "like an army in battle array" (Cant 6:3). Shall a man who has an army of a hundred thousand soldiers around him fear his enemies". A faithful servant of Mary, surrounded by her protection... has still less to fear.

This good Mother..., would rather dispatch battalions of millions of angels to assist one of her servants than that it should ever be said that a faithful servant of Mary, who trusted her, had to succumb to the malice, the number, and the vehemence of his enemies.

**Today's prayer:**

**Come Holy Spirit, living in Mary.**
**Help to praise you for such a quick, easy,**
**and secure path to holiness!**

As I finish this entry I feel the love from Jesus Christ and Mother Mary. I am reminded of a few visions that go along with this lesson. I am asked to record them as I remember them.

A little over a month ago: *I see Mother Mary and she holds an infant child. She is surrounded by fire and I see the serpent surround her feet. Beneath her feet is a darkened crescent moon. The devil is beneath this moon. He reaches up to take this child from Mother Mary. In this vision Mother Mary is calm and sure of herself. I feel the strength and love flow to me. I see cherubs surrounding her in this vision. Love for Mother Mary is felt and seen in this vision.*

I am given tonight the significance of this vision. Why it was brought forward. This child that Mother Mary held from the grasp of the devil was me. I have travelled a long, hard road all my life. Mother Mary has been present and surrounding me all my life. Keeping me strong and safe even though I ran from God and His love and light. Even though I fell carrying very heavy crosses all my life.

Another vision God asks me to share:

I have come to love this Archangel so very much.

Saint Michael has been my protector and guardian angel all my life. He has had a tough job, and I bow to him tonight for loving me through it all.

*I am shown my life as a whole. I have been full of love and light. I have tried my best all my life to love and be-loved. I run and fall. Saint Michael, in this vision picks me up after I fall. Jesus and Saint Michael in this vision take my hands and pull me up after I fall three times. After*

*I end up in a mental facility. Unbalanced, my head was disconnected from my heart. I lost my heart and I fell with the crosses that I have run with all my life.*

*Never a more heart wrenching vision is the sight of Jesus Christ holding me in His own arms after I cross over to the other side. This happened in March of 2012, after a failed gastric by-pass.*

*Jesus holds me, and I see myself lying down. He holds me in His arms. Jesus Christ cries tears of sorrow, and moments later as He kisses me, I come back to life. I received the breath of God through the love of Jesus Christ. His love for me is that strong and beautiful.*

The vision to help me wrap up the *Consecration* word of the day:

*In a dream I see myself and I am just an outlined figure, representing my soul-essence. I then see Mother Mary's soul-essence. Mother Mary melds as one with my own soul. I lie in a tomb and we become one soul and one heart.*

Now we are one in the same physical body. Mother Mary's Immaculate Heart beats strong today within the walls of my own chest. Jesus Christ's own Sacred Heart I feel vibrate and shine in the night. Almost nightly as I sleep, I see the rays shine bright from my own heart. The merging of the Father, Son and Mother of God has become complete.

In helping me to understand all that has transpired through the kiss of death and the breath of life, God has shown me as worthy of all His love. He calls me His greatest miracle of today. I write words of love for God to the Elders of the Catholic Church.

Visions, dreams, and meditations. Bible lessons, invocations, dictionary words, and history lessons all meld together to help secure a future for our children. I record this love affair of God through the love of Jesus Christ and Mother Mary's own power and Divine Mercy!!!

# THE SOUND OF MUSIC

### 'Food for the soul'

8:52 p.m.
November 7, 2017

**Song of the day: Something Good**

### SOMETHING GOOD

*Perhaps I had a wicked childhood*
*Perhaps I had a miserable youth*
*But somewhere in my wicked, miserable past*
*There must have been a moment of truth*
*For here you are, standing there loving me*[60]

Jesus picks this song of the day after I heard a most beautiful song for the day's events. I concede and let His song be placed exactly where He wants it in His books of Revelations. My love affair with the Father and Son of God.

Holding tight tonight to His arm and I hold my breath and Jesus Christ breathes for me. Patience is not my greatest attribute. I only want what God wants. Healing for our children and awareness of God's deep love for each of them.

As I type the lyrics to this song I feel Jesus hold me. He comes around me and I feel the warmth of His arms. His hands rest on my forearms as he encircles me in the chair tonight.

I feel the heat of His deep passion and I could never truly explain the love we feel for one another.

He has loved me all my life. I feel His love tonight and it comes through as an arrow piercing my own heart and soul, a deep, true passion for the love of God.

---

[60] *Something Good,* lyrics, Richard Rodgers.

*Bella Louise Allen*

Poetry goes along with this song. Our hearts' flame is fanned higher the further we walk together.

# HEARTS UNITED

*"Our hearts were created when the Divine shattered*
*Into billions of tiny pieces*
*Little flames and droplets of divinity, that shattered*
*Throughout the universe. Some of these pieces became the sea,*
*Some became fire, some became the trees, and some became souls*
*When two people fall in love that is their spark*
*Of the Divine seeing the other's spark and knowing it*
*And their relationship reunites two pieces of God*
*The moment our eyes met, I knew you*
*The moment our hearts met I knew myself*
*You complete me*
*You are a mirror in which I see all things reflected*
*Let me share myself with you*
*Let me offer myself to you*
*My love, my sweetness, my true one...*
*My heart, my soul, my dear one...*
*We are two rivers flowing into one another*
*We are two hearts beating as one."*

**Unknown Author**

A most beautiful poem, yet not mine. God asks me to share it for it describes the love we hold for one another. It describes the love we hold for the children of the world.

Passion of the Christ. I am in love with the Father and the Son of God. One in the same beings. Energy, Spirit and Love. We three have become One. The Father, Son and The Mother of God!!!

# TRUE LOVES DEVOTION

## The Flames of True Love...

5:26 a.m.
November 10, 2017

I work three jobs for over the past three months as I write monumental books for the love of my life, for Jesus Christ and for the Father. I am a direct support worker for two separate companies. I still run a successful part-time cleaning business.

I try with all my might to continue to work magic for God with the books of new Revelations for the Catholic Church. My will is not my own. Everything I do is for the love of God, who has taken over my entire existence. I love God for all He has given to me.

God tells me, ***"Please, keep your faith. Do not lose heart."***

I hold onto hope. For if I do not, Jesus tells me, ***"It would crush My own heart."***

Over the past two years I have been given history lessons, Bible lessons, dictionary words, invocations, songs and poetry - all for the love of God and our children. God is putting magic to paper through my own hands. He shares with me, ***"The sky is the limit with the love that we write together."***

**Lesson of the day:** Does true love still exist in a world in utter chaos?

I wake throughout the night to the sounds of coughing. The dying woman that I take care of is in the end stages of life. She is a most beautiful soul-piece of the Father's. She is in her late 90's and her candle will soon go out.

She enjoyed a marriage to her own "Twin Flame," her husband of 73 years.

This most beautiful soul has dedicated most of her life to service to others. Her family has always come first. The mother of five beautiful children, she was the wife of a World War II Veteran. He was her sweetheart, a perfect match since their High School days.

This most beautiful couple shares together songs before retiring each night. Her own special Veteran sings her to sleep. This is a special song, for it holds her name within the lyrics. She lights up the moment her husband sings to her, *'If you knew Suzie like I know Suzie'*.

These are Messages from her husband and he speaks of his love for her within the lyrics of this wonderful song. It warms my heart and Jesus' heart as we watch them love one another in her last days.

A most beautiful song this morning. Words of endearment and they are not for me.

Jesus and I watched over the past few weeks. Suzie's own candle, her life, will soon fade.

## IF YOU KNEW SUSIE LIKE I KNOW SUSIE...

*I have got a sweetie known as Susie*
*In the words of Shakespeare; she's a "wow"*
*Though all of you may know her, too*
*I'd like to shout right now*
*Susi has a perfect reputation*
*No one ever saw her on a spree*
*Nobody knows where Susie goes*
*Nobody knows but me*
*If you knew Susie, like I know Susie*
*Oh! Oh! Oh! What a girl*

Moved by this tribute to a beautiful soul on the way to Heaven, I am asked to share the love God holds for this husband and wife. Life's struggles have never held these two down. They forged on and loved one another through it all, year after year. I'm sure they had their own trials. Their love affair began for them in High School.

They were High School sweethearts and the flame they felt has burned bright since the moment they laid eyes on one another. Just like the love of Jesus Christ and myself. Just like the love we could all have.

Susie passed on to Heaven October 27, 2017. May she be enjoying the sunsets from Heaven as she waits for her true love to join her!!!

# IF ONLY THEY HAD HIS BODY!!!

### *'The Father, Son and The Holy Spirit resurrected and walking as One'*

2:58 p.m.
November 11, 2017

**Lessons in deep love:**

Many times, during the thirty years after the crucifixion of the Lord, Jewish leaders would have produced Jesus' body had they been able to do so. On the day of Pentecost and in the aftermath of Peter's inspired sermon, they saw thousands of Jews coming to believe in this resurrected Christ. Had they been able to produce His body, it would have sent most of those converts scurrying back to their synagogues and Christianity would have died right there. Why didn't this happen? Very simply—they didn't have the body!

Immediate growth of the church does in deep support the fact of the resurrection. My point here, however, is that such reasoning—a mere five or six weeks after the crucifixion—would have been unnecessary if the body of Jesus could have been produced. That, however, was impossible, because Jesus had "risen as He said.".

Let's assume that Christ did not rise from the dead. Let's assume that the written accounts of His appearances to hundreds of people are false. I want to pose a question. With an event so well publicized, don't you think that it's reasonable that one historian, one eyewitness, one antagonist would record for all time that he had seen Christ's body: "Listen, I saw that tomb—it was empty! Look, I was there, Christ did not rise from the dead. As a matter of fact, I saw Christ's body." The silence of history is deafening when it comes to testimony against the resurrection.

## Who moved the stone?

The big question is, who rolled away the stone? It couldn't have been His enemies, for as we have seen they made contingency plans to cover up the fact that it had been rolled away and that His body was missing. Outside of the explanation found in the Gospels, there are only two possibilities".

Jesus. Himself woke up from his death and rolled it away. The women or some other friends rolled it away.

Both options are a version of the "swoon theory" or the "resuscitation theory" (both of which are ridiculous and will be dealt with in the next chapter). The first imagines a Jesus so weakened that He couldn't carry His own cross (as a result of His beatings) and then, after hanging on the cross for nine hours and being left for dead by Roman soldiers who were experts at crucifixion (who when thrust a spear into His side so that "blood and water flowed out"). Then miraculously woke up, found Himself tightly wrapped in grave clothes, yet out of them without disturbing their order and proceeded to move a two-ton stone. That would take a bigger miracle than the resurrection!

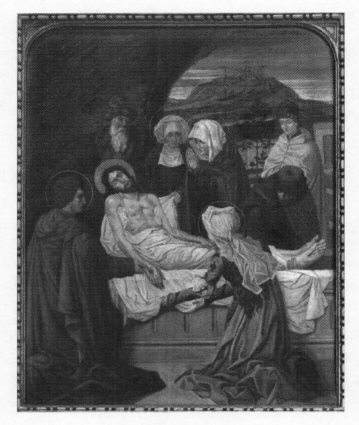

Photo By: Shutterstock

**Message:** As I type these words of contemplation, of "who moved the stone from the tomb where Jesus Christ was laid to rest over 2,000 years ago?" I am shown this vision of Jesus in the tomb: God is present within the tomb. I see God's own LIGHT within the dark walls of the tomb. And from God comes the words, ***"My Son, awaken!"***

I see the pure white light blaze up within the darkness of the closed tomb. I see Jesus' body wrapped in the shroud that He was laid to rest in, according to Jewish law. I see His body that was not prepared with oils herbs because the women had to prepare the feast of Passover. [61]They would bring them in the morning...

---

[61] Biblical refs.

I see Jesus' lifeless body in the tomb.

As God's presence remains in the tomb, I see this shroud that encircles Jesus' body, and it falls away. Jesus finishes removing it from His body. He slowly awakens and removes this material from His body.

Jesus stands within the tomb.

The knowing within my heart and the vision I receive as I type this entry into God's books of Revelations is that God removed the stone from the tomb.

I write; and it is God's own hands that put these words to the paper.

After the stone is removed from the entry of the tomb and the light of dawn comes through the entrance, I see Jesus and He walks out of the tomb. He stands in the light and Jesus falls to His knees and cries in exaltation to Lord and God. *"**Thanks be to God!**"*

I sit and contemplate the meaning of this vision. My heart races to know that something so great has been shared with me. I am asked to take on the role of Mother of God, and to accept the name and identity of God's own wife. Many mysteries and lessons in love have been shared with me through the Grace of God alone.

I receive chills up and down the right side of my body. I feel the excitement of Jesus Christ within me. Knowing and understanding where the books of Revelations are and the great men who will be reading these books someday gives me hope for all that God has shown me. Enlightening the Elders of the Catholic Church with God's own Truths is what He has asked me to do.

As I type the last paragraph my ears become full. I feel the pressure of the Angels and saints within. They all see and feel this excitement of the words put to paper for the Father and Son.

God shares with me the vision of Jesus Christ in the Heavens above after He ascended to the Heavens.

I see Jesus as a beautiful whole man. He wears the purest of white robes, and a radiant purple sachet hangs around His neck. A huge cross of golden threads is embroidered in the center of His robe. He stands in the Heavens above and the brightest white surrounds His entire being.

I see Jesus' Heart today as I sit in the chair and type His words to the screen of my computer. I see Jesus' own Sacred Heart emanating with pure white light beneath my own chest as I write love letters to the Catholic Church for God.

An amazing vision! God is so very beautiful!

My heart starts throbbing with pain as I continue to type. This is proof to me that my eyes and heart belong to God/Jesus and to the Mother of God.

These body pains and sensations do not belong to me. I have given my body to God.

I live, breathe, and cry tears of blood for the Father and the Son of God.

Who moved the stone from the tomb? - Lesson continued:

The other possibility is that the women, who in three of the four Gospel accounts openly asked each other; "who will roll away the stone for us", nevertheless drummed up the strength to open the grave. But even had they managed such thing, that doesn't explain how they could break the Roman seal and do all their work without disturbing the sleeping guards!

I have visited the garden tomb in Jerusalem on six occasions. Although we can't be certain it is the one in which Jesus was buried, it does conform to all the scriptural requirements: It is in a "garden" and is close to the place of the skull where Jesus was crucified "outside the wall" of Old Jerusalem. But even if it isn't the exact tomb, it is typical of those of the period. An eight to ten-inch grove or track running downhill toward the door of the tomb was cut in the rock so that after the body was placed inside, the stone could be rolled down the roove to the block, sealing the tomb entrance. To move the stone—estimated to weigh at least one and halt to two tons—back up the inclined groove the women did not remove the stone. Then who did?

They said a stone of that size would have to have had a minimum weight of 1-1 ½ to 2 tons. No wonder Matthew and Mark said the stone was extremely large.

So, who moved the stone? The Bible has a simple answer, "And behold, there was a great earthquake; for an angel of the Lord descended from heaven and came and rolled back the stone from the door and sat on it.

## Message as I write this entry:

I am reminded of a drawing that I have in my own artwork. Not a very good depiction of the ascension that took place as Jesus' body is resurrected from the dead. [62] I receive pictures to go along with the

---

[62] Jesus ascended later

writings and I usually get the drawings from the spirit world before I work on the lesson that God wants revealed to the Elders of the Catholic Church. God is amazing and this entry into His own books of Revelations is proof of God's true love and the power that Jesus Christ now has through the Father.

I am reminded as I write this entry of the many times Jesus has "lured" me into the tomb where His own body was taken after His crucifixion. I have put ointment on His back, hands and feet to help in His healing from the crucifixion that happened over 2,000 years ago. The vision shows the deep, passionate love that I hold for Jesus Christ, the love and faith that I have for the Creator of the world.

Jesus has taken me to the tomb to make love to Him there more than a few times as well. He sets the scene for our own love affair.

God shares with me in dreams and meditation the love that Jesus held for Mary Magdalene. As I write this entry He shows me through the ecstasy and visions of the love and passion He still feels for her today. The child Sarah that they conceived was true and real. I would never question this love or the truth of God's own love for this woman! [63]

---

[63] footnote the French tradition

# *HIS SPARROW HAS FALLEN*

*The crisp clear fall air has a bite to it this morning.*
*My tears still linger to my cheeks today and I wake*
*from another long night spent loving my Lord.*
*His sparrow has fallen and does not know how to fly…*

12:56 p.m.
December 1, 2017

I haven't written for nearly a month and my heart hurts from all of God's lessons through Jesus Christ's love. He holds me tight this morning and I don't know where to turn. No counsel still from the Catholic Church and no one understands fully all that I have been given by God. A miracle of life after death and God has granted Mother Mary His Divine Mercy. A love story written by the hands of God through the love of Jesus Christ.

The Trinity concept is just the tip of the iceberg of the lessons I have been taught from the Mother, Father and the Son of God. A lost lamb resurrected from a living hell of my own. Given God's own graces and the lesson I have learned most is the deep passionate love that God holds for me as a woman.

Jesus Christ has taken over my entire existence. I wake with His hands upon my body and God vibrates my awake through my brain. I feel the kisses and the love of all the angels and saints as they wake me with music of love and light. Never a more beautiful love affair with the whole spirit world.

I hold tight today to God's promises of love and light for all our children. I let go of the fantasies of a movie, a documentary and even the fantasy of saving the lives of some of our children. God tells me, *"I have this one"*.

He is in control no matter what anyone thinks. His love will prevail over all else in this world. His light will continue to shine throughout eternity. No matter how many sparrows fall to the ground. No matter how young or old. No matter how matter how innocent or naïve. NO matter how deceitful or evil the sparrow. God will reign supreme through it all.

He breathes us in and He breaths us out. One soul at a time.

A disheartening vision comes to me two days ago. I still struggle what to do with it. For nearly two hours I was bombarded with the negative energy force. Fear had taken over and my heart raced, and I felt a deep anger throughout my body. As I work through this fear and anger I seek shelter from the torture that I felt in my own soul. I went to bed to ask for strength from God and I beg for mercy for the overwhelming feelings of fear and anger.

As I lay on my bed and cry tears I hear her come through my heart. These are the words Mother Mary speaks to me as my own heart feels the sharp painful arrows that she feels.

*"Dead sparrows falling everywhere". "Dead sparrows falling everywhere". Dead sparrows falling everywhere".*

These words were repeated for nearly five minutes as tears flow from my eyes. I feel the sharp points of pain through my own heart. I hear these words repeated through my heart. I have the knowing of Mother Mary's presents as I hear these words come from my own heart. I see the dead sparrows laying on the ground.

The sparrows that Mother Mary is speaking of; are not birds with feathers that fly in the sky. The 'sparrows that Mother Mary speaks of is our children. God's own babies. Young and old alike. I see them falling. There are thousands of children laying on the ground. I know the connection with this vision to the words "Dead sparrows falling everywhere".

For over two years God has been revealing the information and warnings of World War III. He has been reaching out to me from the heavens above to connect with me and ask me to love and write His own fears for our children. I am now fully awake to all God's love for our children.

I help God release His fears and His tears. Deep sadness over took me this night. It was not my own feelings of anger and fear, it was the fear of God's and Mother Mary's for the children of the world.

I hold a special place in God's own heart. I am literally being held up by the power of God. The love He holds for me is so very overpowering. Without God's love and power, I would not be breathing air into my own lungs.

The Sparrow has fallen. Mother Mary is here to help raise God up high in the sky.

God shares with me many lessons over the course of this journey. I fall from grace by running from God's love and in my own deepest *"darkest night of the soul"* I fall, and God saves me from death. Mother Mary's pure heart cleanses my own heart. I am given life from the Father, Son and the Mother of God.

Brought back to life for a special project and for saving lost souls of the world.

I will continue, my Lord to love you as a true wife would. I will continue to write your love, hope and dreams for all our children. I will hold tight to my waist and feel your deep passionate love as you hold me in the same moments. Our mind, body and spirit have merged. I am a most humble and blessed woman of God.

## *FOOTPRINTS IN THE SAND*

*I walk along the beach alone; no one in sight*
*Time matters not to me, as I stroll the*
*distance in the beautiful sunlight*
*The foot prints in the sand I leave behind me today are deep*
*Larger than they should be*
*I walk with a heavy heart and Jesus walks with me*

*Sharing His own tears and fears for the children of the world*
*His heart skips a beat and I feel it within my own*
*The love I have given to Him compares to no other love*
*The memories we have shared turned back the clock of time*
*To another life; another time*
*Tears of blue and blood drips down His brow in too many of*
*These memories He shares with me*
*The footprints in the sand I see fill with His own blood today*
*Painful to see the grains of sand within these footprints behind*
*Me turn to a deep crimson red*
*He hopes for a brighter future*
*He hopes for a better world*
*An enlightened child of God*
*Sent back to the world; a miracle of God's own*
*To spread His deep messages of true love*
*To spread His words of forgiveness and love*
*These footprints in the sand are deep today...*

# BROKEN HEARTED

*His love is evident throughout history and Jesus'
Temple shuts out God's own love and light.*

6:44 p.m.
December 2, 2017

Another busy day walking and loving with Jesus Christ. The sky is a clear blue with a few light fluffy clouds. I work early today as usual and God tests me again today.

*"How much do you love me"?* Words that Jesus asks me several times over the course of this journey, walking as one with Him.

Today I find out how dedicated I am to the Creator of the world. His projects are at a standstill and I hold tight to Jesus' hand. A package from the Diocese. As I open it I wonder what Monsignor's response will be. It has been nearly two and a half months since our last conversation. Monsignor 'D' asked me to give him the weekend to pray and meditate on our conversation and it has been seventy-two days. I have called twice since then and left two messages for a call back.

I find out today that the books that I have written as I hold Jesus' hand for the past two years have not been opened and the Catholic Church will not be reading any of them. God's own heart lays on the floor. I feel my own hopes for helping to bring love, light, faith and hope to the world, crumble to the ground. God has assured me His books would make a difference. He assures me that His bringing me back to life would make a change of love happen for many of our children.

Tears flow from my eyes and I try to catch my breath several times today. I still hold on to my own reality.

Living in the spirit world most days with Jesus and the angels and saints is so very hard to do. I try with all my might to stay in my own reality. I work and strive to be in the perfect likeness of God each day. Shining a bright light becomes more difficult some days. Today was one of those hard days for me.

I have sought long and hard for counsel from Jesus' own church, the Catholic Church. I first reached out to Father 'M' at Saint John's on August 28, 2016. I was already writing books with Jesus for a year. Learning to love straight from my heart and follow the breath of God has not been easy.

Dreams of epic proportions brought to me straight from the Father and as I hold Jesus' hand daily now I see and feel all His love. Deep passionate love of God is felt with only a thought or a song on the radio. Never a more romantic man, have I known in all my life.

Today Jesus teaches me patience once again. It has already been over two years since He brought me a sweet angel from the other side. He placed her in my lap and asked me to walk and talk with Him while He taught me how to wrap my brain around my new journey. My soul-purpose

Is to write books of love, light, faith and hope and I believe I have done that to the best of my abilities.

I thought God wanted the Catholic Churches approval for the books that we write together. I thought He wanted them to reap the rewards of this great love story. I thought they could help me to put only the best parts of God's own love affair to book form and then to movie.

Raising money through the love and light that is being portrayed through the books that we write together for awareness of God's own truths. Raising money to help with so many issues that have been devastating all of God's children around the world. I now wonder, where He will lead me?

Photo by: Shutterstock

*A sweet angels wishes were given to St. Julie Ann in October of 2015. The 'innocent children' of the world who suffer greatly today is why she continues to forge on in the wilderness to help those in need of love, light, faith and hope!*
*This sweet angel sleeping is in representation of "Sweet Little Miss Felicia"; an angel whose candle was blown out far too soon! Her wishes from heaven are to share her love story with her mother and the children of the world who are taken from this world by choices beyond their own control! Innocent and precious gifts given to all of us, sent from Heavens doors straight into our arms from the Creator; Himself!*

### AN ANGELS CHRISTMAS WISH
*An angel in pink stands in the distance*
*Bent over tying the laces of her ballet shoes*
*She hears her name, "Miss Felicia"*
*She twirls and sees Mother Mary coming towards her*
*The excitement can be seen in her sparkling blue eyes*
*The moment has arrived for her story to be shared.*
*A gift to her mother, six years in the making.*
*The package is wrapped*
*Gift wrapping of white with a ribbon of red*
*Ready for her mommy to see her whole story of heavens surprises.*
*Mary bends down and asks her; "are you ready my darling"?*
*"Your mommy has been so sad".*

157

> *"Your books of love from the other side*
> *Is your gift to her from the heavens above".*
> *Little Miss Felicia smiles and takes Mother Mary's hand*
> *To the edge of the beach they stroll.*
> *They see Jesus waiting,*
> *To present this sweet angel's Christmas Wish*
> *To her mother below!*

# HIS OCEAN OF MERCY

### *The tears we shed fill the ocean blue*

2:44 a.m.
December 3, 2017

I try to rest tonight, and Jesus wakes me early this morning. Over an hour ago I feel God vibrate me awake. Restless in the early hours of the morning and He wants to talk. As I hold Jesus close this morning and we talk as one through the Father and Mother I am shown an ocean of the deepest blue water.

Saint John Paul II has taught me of the Ocean of Mercy that God gives to His children. He has taught me to be patient and Mother Mary reminds me to be kind and loving to all God's children. Some days that is harder than others; but her pure heart is that of my own today.

God reminds me this morning of His own deep passionate love for me. I feel the light kisses as we share love this morning as we converse. He is not going to leave me. I love Him so, for that reminder. My own heart is full of deep sadness. Sadness; since the church that was founded after Jesus Christ's crucifixion won't and can't see the love that He tries to portray for all our children through the books that I write for Him.

Lessons in love, faith and hope and the Catholic Church continues to hide behind their own guilt and shame.

Photo By: Shutterstock

*Jesus watches over the children. God knows all and sees all.*
*It is through our own eyes He sees the devastation first hand.*
*"Through Me, with Me, in Me, in the Unity of the Holy Spirit".*

Jesus and I talk about G. P. this morning. A very sensitive subject for the Catholic Church. One in many that God knows of. Deep pain comes forward with this conversation and it is proof of Mother Mary's and Jesus' own ocean of tears.

God sees all and knows all. He shares with me the guilt of Mr. P.'s indiscretions on the lives of the innocent children. A most horrible subject and that is the innocent lives of so many of God's own children being subject to child molestation and abuse. Just one of the reasons God chose me for His own wife this time around. Experience with so many issues that He and our children need help with.

Moving past the pain to heal. I have done that with my own father. Forgiving the people in our lives that do wrongs to us. My own father was a very wounded and sick man at the time of his own indiscretions towards me. I understand this, and my heart still feels the pains for his wrong doings to me. Memories that will never go away. However, they have faded as I see the other side of the coin (if you will). My own father's traumas and dramas that caused him to be and act the way he did. Not an excuse for his behavior but an understanding to it all.

Jesus talks straight forward with me about all things. Something I truly wish someone in the real world would do. Something I wish I could seek and find counsel for. Someone from the Catholic Church.

God knows my heart is heavy from the burden of all the visions He has shown me. Prophecy from the Bible and the lives of the past angels who have fallen and not been able to make it into heaven. God's own children who wander in the 'purgatory' that the Catholic Church speaks of.

These lost souls reach out to me for prayers and guidance the closer I walk with Jesus.

My body pains me greatly this morning. Tears that I have not yet cried. Emotions that lay just under the surface of my burdened heart.

I discuss tonight the fact that I haven't even fully cried the death of my father. Back in August of 2013. I watched my own father suffer greatly before God took his soul to heaven. A process that would not have happened, had it not been for my sister being diligent and getting my father baptized and getting is own heart in the right place with God. It is never too late to bring a lost soul out of its wounded and lost state.

I witnessed along with my whole family the angels trying to take my father to the heavens above. An amazing memory for my family.

God said; *"Not yet"*. My father continued to breath for nearly twenty-four hours after that. We, as a family saw the angels trying to carry him to heaven. God waited for my father's last rites with Father 'P'. Something I had never witnessed before.

Time is so very precious to all of us. Something God reminds me of this morning. We are all here only for a blink of an eye.

\*

*God's Promises*
*To love and to honor until death do us part*
*Our hearts beat as one and I feel the deep love of Jesus Christ*
*His love no longer can be denied*
*His promises to never leave me are evident within the night*
*His Sacred Heart shines bright from my own Immaculate Heart*
*Shining in the night and we grow closer every day*

# HEAVENLY PRAYERS

## *The angels on high pray on bended knee*
## *for the children of the world*

3:33 p.m.
December 4, 2017

God's love holds me up daily now. The life force of the angels and saints is felt stronger and Jesus Christ loves me so for all I have done. Books written and God's love for His children is evident throughout each page.

I am still tested daily. Jesus loves me so for not losing faith. He loves me so for my own faith in God's power in love.

I feel Mother Mary's presence strong today. I am grateful for her when I feel her step forward. My own mother is not prepared to support me. I hold tight to Jesus daily for strength and love. My own reality is the spirit world. Taken over by the grace of God and my dreams are filled with God's love. Messages throughout the night and then the angels wake me with love songs.

God vibrates me awake and Jesus touches my heart with His deep love for me.

Today however, Mother Mary shows me her love and support. I cry tears with her and she knows my heart is heavy with all that God has asked of me. Understanding the lessons of what happened to me in March of 2012 has been difficult. The word 'ascension' is brought to me again today by Mother Mary.

I have seen my own angel-self in the heavens above. In the bedchambers with Jesus Christ. Mother Mary has vibrated out of my own body and I see my soul-essence stand with Mother Mary.

Seeking counsel again today and I am guided to reach out this morning as I walk out of Saint Mary's Catholic Church. I approach Father 'B', a young priest who speaks in place of God.

I speak to him this morning and find out he will only be with the parish for two more weeks. I tell him of my heavy heart and how I feel I'm in need of counsel for all that God has been bringing to me. I touch base on the books that I have written for God. I talk of how I walk daily with Jesus. I tell him about the length of time I have already been reaching out to Father 'M' and the fact that I have reached out to the Diocese.

Father 'B' takes my information is as we speak. I see in his eyes the understanding of the heaviness that I am feeling in my heart. He asks me for my name and telephone number and I give it to him. He tells me he will pass this information on to Father "I".

So, I wait for word from the Catholic Church again. I wait for direction from God. I hold tight to Jesus' arm and we will walk, talk, sing and love one another as a real husband and wife. My heart is immersed in the love of God. I know, no matter what happens God has me. I know that the angels and saints love me. I know that Mother Mary supports all that I do, for she portrayed that most of the morning through the tears and love she showered me with after mass.

## GOD'S LOVE AND JOY

### *Jesus Christ is present within and I feel His immense love this morning*

8:13 a.m.
December 5, 2017

Tears of frustration are felt this morning and God loves me so for all my devotion and the passionate love I shower Him with. "Divine Mercy" at its greatest has been granted to the "Mother of God". Risen from the dead and a love brought back to life through my own body.

> **Word of the day: Lamentation**-the passionate expression of grief or sorrow, weeping, scenes of lamentation.".
>
> Synonyms-weeping, wailing, sobbing, moaning, lament, keening, grieving, mourning. "the survivor's lamentation".

A book of the Bible telling of the desolation of the Judah after the fall of Jerusalem in 586 BC. "the act of lamenting or expressing grief. 2. Lament. 3. Lamentations, (used with singular verb) a book of the Bible, traditionally ascribed to Jeremiah."

**What is the purpose of a prayer of lamentation?**

"Lament is a tool that God's people use to navigate pain and suffering. Lament is a vital prayer for people of God because it enables them to petition for God to help deliver from distress, suffering and pain. Lament prayer is designed to persuade God to act on the sufferer's behalf.

One night many months ago, after too many tearful nights spent loving my Lord. He walks me back in time and I am taken to the Wailing Wall. I have no knowledge of the meaning behind this Wailing Wall when Jesus Christ takes me here to teach me of God's own sorrows for the children of the world. After writing books of epic proportions for my Creator I now understand why He took me to this place.

God is on His knees for a world in turmoil. His children are shutting His love and light out and there is no other way to bring them home than through this tragedy.

**History of the Wailing Wall:**

"The term "Wailing Wall" is almost exclusively used by Christians. It was revived in the period of non-Jewish control between the establishment of British Rule in 1920 and the Six-Day War in 1967. The term "Wailing

Wall" is not used by Jews and increasing not by many others who consider it derogatory."

"The Western Wall, Hebrew also called Wailing Wall. It is located in the Old City of Jerusalem, a place of prayer and pilgrimage sacred to the Jewish people. It is the only remains of the Second Temple of Jerusalem, held to be uniquely holy by the ancient Jews and destroyed by the Romans in 70 ce."

\*

After another tearful morning spent loving my husband. An amazing man loved by so many and I am graced daily with His own passionate side. Our love and joy is felt this morning even though I cry tears of deep sadness this morning.

We prepare to put our first two books written together, as husband and wife, into production. Jesus Christ has taken over my entire existence and this morning Mother Mary steps forward and loves with me. I feel her stronger every day as I walk holding Jesus' hand. Some days I don't recognize her presence within for God tells me I am her and she is me.

His own love and joy is shown this morning after we love one another. I feel as if I have failed Him repeatedly and He assures me I have not failed Him in the least. Our books were meant for the children of the world and God knew the Catholic Church would shut His love out. He knew I would have to pick up and move on from His own Temple.

The very reason He chose me and loves me is I "believe in things seen and unseen". Something the Catholic Church was speaking of just a few weeks back. My own death and resurrection is just one of the lessons God has tried to convey through our love story. A miracle for the Catholic Church and a miracle for the children of the world. I hold tight to His hand and we will be great no matter where He leads me with our love story.

# HIS SACRED HEART FADES

*His heart bleeds a deep red*
*I see it, dripping slowly as I close my eyes*
*Visions in the night and Jesus Christ reaches out to me*
*As each day passes His heart fades*
*God's children close their eyes to His love*
*His sacrifice forgotten and faded*
*Tears too many fall, all around Him*
*Sad and lonely He waits in the light*
*On His knees today begging*
*"Please open your hearts"*
*"Let me in"*
*"Let me lead you"*
*Fire reigns down, evil and anger have weakened*
*His own heart today*
*Choices made against God's own love*
*His most innocent children pay the ultimate price*
*Truths since the beginning of time hidden in riddles and parables*
*Passages in God's greatest books ever written*
*Dusty and with faded pages*
*Yellowed from too much time gone by*
*History made too many times, wounds and battle scars resurfaced*
*Jesus Christ's Sacred Heart yearns*
*For the love of all God's children to turn to Him for love and guidance*
*His Sacred Heart fades....*

As we write this book of love, light, faith and hope our hearts are filled with sorrow for the children of the world who suffer greatly today. Hoping to spread the word of God's saddened heart through these series of books. Never a more powerful message of love has been written before.

# Book Two

## Love Everlasting

Photo By: Shutterstock

***The Ascension of Jesus Christ***
***"Christ is Truly Ascended into Heaven. We believe that our
Lord Jesus Christ, in his same flesh, ascended above all visible
heavens into the highest heaven, that is, the dwelling-place of
God and the blessed ones, at the right hand of the Father".***

# OUR LADY OF LOURDES

### *"And the waters gushed forth like a spring"*

5:14 p.m.
December 6, 2017

It's bitterly cold tonight as I look back at all that God has given me. The snow falls gently outside my window and the tears come and go again today. Contemplating today; I think of God's great love that He holds for me. Wondering where He will lead me with all His magnificent books.

We love each other today fully like a true husband and wife. Gods own heart keeps me going strong. I feel the kisses of the angels within on and off as we listen to the songs of an amazing soul-piece of the Fathers. Music to help keep our love alive and Johnny Cash was God's own choice for the day.

Johnny Cash was a wounded child and a lost soul finding his own way in the world. So much tragedy and so much love all in one amazing man. Johnny Cash changed the lives and outlook of many. He shared his own passions and love of God through music. He was a man I always could relate to. He reminded me so much of my own father. Trauma's and drama's, they both lived through and still they both made it through the gates of Heaven.

As God and I reflect today on all the love we have for one another, He asks me to write again about an amazing Saint. One that God tells me' *"You, my love; were Saint Bernadette"*. Proving life after death and that is just one of the deep lessons in love that God has portrayed through the books that we write together.

Choosing the perfect woman to be the "Handmaid of the Lord" and Jesus Christ tells me Mother Mary chose me to be this woman. To be like her. To fill in for her and to love her own Son more than any other woman ever has. Mother Mary tells me I am her greatest miracle. To accept and love God fully into my heart, is 'amazing grace' in itself.

*Bella Louise Allen*

## Revisiting the "Waters at Lourdes"

Many people over the centuries have visited the caves at Grotto. This is a place I would love to go back to.

God shares with me a very special jar of hearts. He tells me to fill this jar of hearts with the hearts and lives that I have lived. It starts in this lifetime with my own pure heart. That of Saint Julie Ann. Born on July 21, 1967. He then shares with me Saint Faustina is my next heart to place in this very special jar. The heart that God shares with me today; **"Please accept this heart as one of your own". "You were the precious Saint Bernadette; at the cave in Grotto".**

One of the reasons God loves me so much is; I believe in all He gives me. Jesus Christ holds my hand strong today and He tells me God's love for me has been burning strong since before the beginning of time. He tells me I was His Eve in the Garden of Eden and I believe.

God tells me my pure heart and my innocent child-like love for life is why He loves me so. Keeping and staying young at heart in these trying times can be very hard to do. Leading from the heart and I have always done just that.

I am told that Saint Bernadette was a gentle soul Full of love and her own heart was my own. Soul-pieces of the Father and no one knows God's children better than God; Himself.

The water at Lourdes was thought to have healing powers and God shares with me the meaning behind the water at Lourdes. Today as we love like a true husband and wife He shares with me the connection between my own tears and the waters at the feet of Mother Mary at the cave in Grotto.

"Living waters" is a representation of healing tears. Mother Mary and I cry tears through my body and they belong to God. I have cried so many tears over the course of this journey with Jesus Christ, God and Mother Mary. Each day I cry for them and with them.

As God brings forward the past, He shares with me the meaning of all the lessons He has taught me. This lesson for Saint Bernadette was in preparation for the lessons God is teaching me today. I cleanse out the tears for God and Mother Mary through my own eyes. I am brought vision after vision daily. Deep sadness is felt through my own heart. Painful body memories are reminders of my walk as one with the Father and Mother of God.

I am told that my destiny since the beginning of time was to be the "New Mary". Time is a continuum and God has proven that through the lessons in deep love that He shares with me. I have helped God's own heart beat stronger today because of the deep love and faith I continue to have in His own power and love.

Showing God's own love for Saint Bernadette today and He reminds me of the promise that Mother Mary gave to Saint Bernadette. *"I do not promise to make you happy in this world, but the next".*

As I come to understand all the lessons God places in front of me I know only one thing. Without the love and power of God I would not be here. I believe in the great miracle of God's own breath bringing me back to life. I believe that Jesus Christ holds me up strong from the inside out. I believe that Mother Mary has cleansed my heart and continues to speak words through my hands and I feel the love of the angels and saints within as the kisses from God. Ecstasy felt only when God finds me worthy of His own deep passionate love.

Jesus Christ asks me today; *"Are you happy, my love?"*

I tell Him, I am the happiest woman alive. To be held up by the power of God and to be fully engulfed in His deep passionate love is a fairy tale like no other.

My strength and perseverance, comes straight from the Creator of the world. I keep up with all my obligations in the real world, and still forging on. I follow the breath of God daily. Helping God to prove His greatest miracle of today and He asks me to keep faith in the

Catholic Church. He asks me to not give up hope for Saint Francis would absolutely love my faith and devotion to Jesus Christ and the Father.

Photo By: Shutterstock

*The Grotto hides an immense immeasurable, treasure. During the ninth apparition, "the Lady" asked Bernadette to scrape the soil, saying to her: "Go to the spring, drink of it and wash yourself there". By these actions, the mystery of the heart of Jesus is revealed for us: "A soldier pierced his heart with his lance and there immediately flowed out blood and water". The herbs and the mud represent the heart of man wounded by sin. However, in the deepest recesses of that heart, there lies the very life of God signified by the Spring. Bernadette asked:" Did the 'Lady' say anything to you?" She replied: "Yes, from time to time, she said: Penance, penance, penance", one must understand, "conversion". For the Church, conversion consists of turning one's heart towards God and towards our brothers and sisters, as Christ taught us.*

# PARTNERS IN CHIRST

*It is important for you to understand that the love you feel*
*for each other needs to be grounded in agape love. This love*
*is the 'Absolute' and comes directly from God; there is no*
*substitute for it, and you could never create it on your own...*
*We have then, two loves that merge into one to bless*
*our life together; absolute love and belonging love.*
*Both need to be at the heart of a relationship.*
*By Ed Wheat*

2:44 a.m.
December 6, 2017

---

**Word of the day: Agape love-** "**Agape** (ancient Greek, agape) is a Greco-Christian term referring to love, "the highest form of love, charity" and "the love of God for man and of man for God'... Within Christianity, agape is the love originating from God or Christ for mankind."

**What is agape love in marriage?** "Agape love is stuff that holds a marriage together—and a family—together through all kinds of seasons. It's the selfless, unconditional type of love that helps people forgive one another, to respect one another, and to serve one another, day in and day out."

---

As I come to understand the deep love God has for me we research the deep meaning behind agape love. God's love is truly unconditional and everlasting. Over the past few years I have come to learn this truth about God on a personal level.

Jesus Christ holds me up from the inside out and I walk daily holding His hand. He reminds me this morning of the love He has always held for me. God asks me daily to remember His sacrifice and all that it has meant over the centuries. Forgiveness of sins and a reminder of His deep passionate love for all the children of the world.

As we come to the end of another year; God shares with me many things. Deep passionate love for all His children is the grandest lesson in the scheme of all the Revelations He has given me. Learning of God's deep seeded love for our children, and His heart lays on the floor and He has asked me to help Him revive His own heart by coming forward with our own love story.

Never in the history of mankind has God taken over the mind, body and spirit of another living soul like He has mine. He calls me Mary and I accept this role of the Mother of God. The woman who gave birth to His only begotten Son.

Our own love will last throughout eternity.

Lessons in the Trinity. Lessons in God's power and love for all our children. I hold tight to His hand daily as we prove the miracle of my own resurrection. Life after death and God loves me so for believing in all that He gives me.

Special songs to help keep our hearts light and connected fully and God tells me this one song was especially created for our own love story. An amazing man and a beautiful soul-piece of the Fathers; creates magic through music.

**Song of the day: Perfect**

### PERFECT
*I found a love for me*
*Darling just dive right in*
*And follow my lead*
*Well I found a girl beautiful and sweet*
*I never knew you were someone waiting for me*
*'Cause we were just kids when we fell in love*
*Not knowing what it was*

**Song writers: Edward Sheeran/Matthew Sheeran**

An amazing husband, friend and lover. Jesus Christ has never portrayed to the children; His deep passionate side. Through our love story He shows just how romantic He can be. Loving and sweet and He tells me repeatedly; *"I am yours and you are Mine"*.

We dance in the kitchen and our hearts overflow with love whenever Ed Sheeran's voice comes over the radio with this beautiful love song. Our hearts truly beat as one and our love is everlasting!

## *DOLCE VERGINE MARIA*

*I TUOI OCCHI BRILLANC D'ADMORE*
*COME IL RAGGIO DI LUNA PI'U LUMINOSO*
*NEL BUIO CIELO NOTTURNO*
*VERGINE MARIA'S DOLCE SORRISO DOLCE CATTURA*
*IL MIO CUORE OGNI VOLT*
*CHE GUARDA LA MIA STRADA*
*LE SU MANI MI TOCCANO DELICATAMENTE*
*IL MIO SACRD CUORE SALTA*
*UN BATTITO OGNI VOLTA*
*LEI SUSSURA DI AMARTI*
*LA MIA DOLCE VERGINE MARIA IL TUO*
*PURO CUORE MI HA SALVATO OGGI*
*I NOSTRIL BATTONO COME*
*UNA VERA VITA*
*DALL'INIZIA DEI*
*TEMPI UN AMORE ETERNO*
*PER TUTTA L'ETERNITI'A*
*LA MIA DOLCE VEERGINE MARIA*

Jesus Christ wakes me early this morning and asks me to write a poem with Him. As I sit and write I am guided by Saint John Paull II to translate this lesson in love from English into Italian. Over the course of this journey angels within teach me lessons. I have dreams in Spanish and Saint Margaret Mary has been teaching me the beautiful language of French.

This morning however I am asked to do a beautiful love poem from Jesus Christ's own Sacred Heart to my Immaculate Heart; in the language of Italian. I will translate the words spoken to me back into English. The way Jesus Christ wrote this poem to me. An amazing lover, friend and husband this morning.

## SWEET VIRGIN MARY

*YOUR EYES SHINE LOVE*
*LIKE THE BRIGHTEST MOON BEAM IN*
*THE DARK NIGHT SKIES*
*VIRGIN MARY'S SWEET SMILE*
*CAPTURES MY HEART EACH TIME SHE GLANCES MY WAY*
*HER HANDS TOUCH ME SO GENTLY*
*MY SACRED HEART SKIPS A BEAT*
*EACH TIME SHE WHISPERS, "I LOVE YOU, MY LORD"*
*MY SWEET VIRGIN MARY YOUR OWN PURE HEART*
*HAS SAVED ME TODAY*
*OUR HEARTS BEAT AS ONE*
*TRUE LOVE SINCE THE BEGINNING OF TIME*
*A LOVE EVERLASTING THROUGHOUT ETERNITY*
*MY SWEET VIRGIN MARY*

As I finish this poem and see the deep love God has for Mother Mary I see the love that Jesus Christ has for me. God shares many lessons with me over the course of this journey.

God tells me we are like peas in a pod. There is my vessel of pure love and then underneath all my beauty is God, Mother Mary and Jesus Christ. The angels and saints that make up who I am live within me. That is the *'Life force of God'*. That is what makes me unique and amazing.

I have been given the keys to God's own heart. I have been given Divine Mercy by the Father and Mother of Heaven. Jesus Christ's own heart beats beneath my chest and Mother Mary's Immaculate Heart has cleansed and purified me through and through.

My consciousness is one with the Fathers. His deep seeded love for me is evident throughout all the love letters that we write. A love affair that surpasses all the rest. The love of God for the love of the children of the world.

# HOUSE OF THE RISING SON

*"Come unto me; I will lead the way".*

4:44 a.m.
December 7, 2017

## *COME TO THE RIVER*

Come to the river
Come to the river
Come to the river with me
Sit by my side and let's rest awhile
Come to the river with me
Let's talk of the past
Let's release all your tears
Come to the river with me
I know your heart and feel your sadness
Come to the river with me
Come to the river and sit awhile with me
Come to the river and let's move past fear
Let it all go and let me walk with you
Come to the river and dive right in
Let me cleanse those tears and wash them away
Come to the river and free your tears
Come to the river and love with me
Come to the river and be new
Come to the river and love anew...

A poem I write as I hold John the Baptist's hand. Jesus stands within and I feel the love of John the Baptist this morning. I love when I recognize the angels that surround and make up who I am. This morning John holds my hand and we write a poem of Baptism. Cleansing one's soul and heart of its heavy burdens. Letting fear go and joining in the walk of love. Holding all the angel's hands and diving in is another vision from the beginning of my journey and I jumped from the heaven's above and came back just for that purpose. Sharing God's deep love for all the children of the world. To help raise the children of the world's spirits. To help walk gently; and to teach those who are willing; the love and forgiveness that Jesus Christ and God have for all the children of the world. Opening your hearts, let Him lead the way to Salvation and you will feel His love and you can be His love…

# 'MOTHER OF MANKIND'

## *"Come near my children; do not be afraid."*

4:43 p.m.
December 8, 2017

I have been given the keys to God's own heart. Secrets revealed, and I have opened many doors. None as sacred as the secrets of Heaven and Earth.

God tells me, *"You are the Queen of the South"*. He tells me, *"You have risen from a hell of your own"*. Christ holds me from the inside out and I meet angels and saints daily now. I am given names, messages of deep love and inspiring meanings behind who I am and what my soul purpose has always been.

Mother Mary has cleansed my own heart and keeps me strong every day. The further I walk as one with the Father, Son and the Mother of God I am taught great lessons of God's pure love for all the children of the world.

Apparitions throughout history and God connects the meaning behind this apparition to my own journey. *Our Lady of La Salette* is a Marian apparition reported by two children, in Fallavaux, France, In 1846. "Secrets" revealed to Maximin Giraud and Melanie Calvat and their names were brought forward to me by the grace of God two days before I research to find out who they are and what God needed me to know about them.

We are living in trying times today. A lesson God shares with me is yet again, history in the making. The visions and dreams God shares with me will make history. He shares with me daily, as I cry tears of deep sorrow for Him and Mother Mary; that the children of the world are in need of a resurrecting of their own.

Jesus Christ's Sacred Heart bleeds a bright red today and His own pain is felt through my own flesh. Memories of His own crucifixion are brought forward. Mother Mary's deep sorrowful heart is felt through my own heart.

God tells me no other woman has loved Him the way I do. Mind, body and spirit. I have opened myself up completely to all His deep seeded love, and passionate heart.

I have had many visions as I walk with Jesus Christ. I have even seen my own soul-essence standing with Mother Mary in the Heavens above. Deep sadness comes to me with this vision, only because God tells me; ***"You have been, were angels trod"***.

Never a more precious gift then to be given "life after death". A resurrecting of my own soul and God has overshadowed my own lost soul. He found me worthy of helping the children of the world, walk out of fear and into the light of God.

I am a woman of love. I am a woman with much experience and God has formed and molded me into the greatest likeness of Himself. Strong and willful. Kind and loving. Giving of self, to the very end.

Tonight, God shares with me I am His 'New Mary'. I am His Eve from the Garden of Eden. I am His most precious Son who gave up His own life on the cross so long ago.

Today at St. Mary's Catholic Church I feel the nails in my feet again. Not as painful as they were as I hung from the cross.

The vision God shares with me today at Church is Jesus Christ's Sacred Heart nailed to the cross and the nail is rusty and old. Painful and heart breaking. To ask nothing more of His children than to open their hearts and let Him lead them to greatness.

Health and wellness of the mind, body and spirit can be given to each of God's children if they only open their hearts to His deep passionate love.

181

I pray again today. "The Divine Mercy" prayer. I pray the "Hail Mary" prayer and I still wait for the Catholic Church to open their hearts to God's love that He portrays through our books of love, light, faith and hope.

God asks me to present His books one last time to Father 'M', at Saint John's Church. I will do as I am directed. I will do all that God asks me. I will continue to love Jesus to the fullest every day.

I pray tonight for the children of the world. I will bend down on my tired knees and ask again for 'Mercy my Lord, for the children of the world."

*

*Many tearful nights have come and gone! I work tirelessly to get God's books of love, light, faith and hope to the Catholic Church and to the children of the world. I fall behind on my writings and I add additional writings after the "newest" tragedies unfold! Prophecy from the Bible and I have seen these next pages that you the reader will see and feel again too many times! History repeating itself and God's children fall to their knees. Some continue to run in fear and hate! God begs you all to 'STOP', to love one another!*

# DIVINE MERCY

*I will praise the, O Lord, with my whole heart; I will shew forth all thy marvelous works!*

10:15 a.m.
February 8, 2018

The beginning of another day and winter seems to drag on. The cold breeze blows past my face today and I feel the light rain come down on me. The love of God is ever present today and Jesus Christ holds me tight this morning as we go to church.

I receive His love strong at mass and as I close my eyes I am shown the most beautiful miracle of all. No miracle could be more profound than the wounds of Saint John Paul II. His gunshot wounds when the attempt on his life was prophesied and then it came to be.

God reminds me of who I am this morning as I sit at Saint John's Catholic Church. He asks me to take on the role; and stand in today, for Mother Mary. Jesus shares with me I am the "Mother of Mankind". I am His "New Mary". Brought back to life by the power of God's breath. To help raise our children out of the living hell that they have created on their own.

As I am shown Saint John Paul II's gunshot wounds this morning, I see the 'light' that guides these bullets. I see the flesh of Saint John Paul II and I see the bullets just as they enter his vital organs. I am given confirmation of Mother Mary's miracle with saving a great man's life. The closest figure in history to the Son of God!

Saint John Paul II was pure of heart and soul from the beginning to the end. A true light of God. A gift given to the world and he performed great works all the days of his life. A miracle of a man, sent straight from the Heavens above. To help lead God's children to greatness!

God reminds me of His own marvelous works throughout history. The conception of Jesus Christ was God's greatest miracle after the Creation of the world and the first human beings given life.

Today He reminds me of the miracle and love He has performed through my own body. Life after death and I am God's own chosen wife. Brought back to life to help Jesus Christ in His own darkest hours!

God shares with me the importance today of our own love affair. It is the union of the Father, Son and Mother of God. He holds me tighter than He has ever held another human being. I am taught the great love He holds for the children of the world through history lessons, prophecy, verses in the Bible, dictionary words and beautiful songs.

I am reminded of the great love God held for Saint John Paul II this morning. After God shares with me the vision of Saint John Paul II's bullet wounds, He asks me to research the events. I do all that I do for the love of God and the children of the world.

### *The Miracle of Mother Mary*
### *God's Ocean of Mercy for Saint John Paul*
### *II, through the love of Mother Mary*

**The first assassination attempt:**

Date: May 13, 1981, 37 years ago

Non-fatal injuries:3

Location: St. Peter's Square, Vatican City

Weapons: Browning Hi-Power

On May 13th, they sat in the square, writing postcards waiting for the Pope to arrive. When the Pope passed through an adoring and excited crowd of supporters. Agca fired four shots at 17:17 with a 9mm Browning Hi-Power semi-automatic pistol and critically wounded him. He fled the scene as the crowd was in shock and disposed of the pistol by throwing it under a truck, but was grabbed by Vatican Security chief Camillo Cibin, a nun, and several spectators who prevented him from firing more shots or escaping, and he was arrested. All four bullets hit John Paul II; two of them lodged in his lower intestine while the other two hit his left index finger and right arm and injured two bystanders; Ann Odre, of Buffalo New York, was struck in the chest, and Rose Hall was slightly wounded in the arm. The Pope was immediately rushed to the hospital while the authorities combed the site for evidence. Celik panicked and fled without setting off his bomb or opening fire.

On June 26, 2000 Pope John Paul II released the "Third Secret of Fatima" in which he said that Agca's assassination attempt was the fulfillment of this secret. May 13 (the date of the assassination attempt) is the anniversary date of the first apparition of the Virgin Mary to the children of Fatima, something the Pope has always regarded as significant, attributing his survival on that day to her protection. Some doubt the church's full disclosure of the contents of this Secret, believing that it actually predicted the Apocalypse. While in prison on remand, Agaca was widely reported to have developed an obsession with Fatima and during that trial claimed that he was the Second Coming of Christ and called on the Vatican to release the Third Secret.

**The Miracle of Mother Mary-** Saint John Paul II was convinced that Mary, in the form of Our Lady of Fatima, had personally redirected the bullet that hit him, saving his life. He gave a bullet recovered from the Pope-mobile to the local bishop of Fatima, who placed it in the crown of the official image of Mary in the shrine at Fatima, which Pope Francis will venerate.

A year after the first assassination attempt, John Paul II visited Fatima to give thanks to the Virgin for preserving his life.

*

As I walk with Christ daily; God has proven His love for the children of the world. The love He holds for Saint John Paul II is so very evident with this history lesson. Evil lurks within the world today and God will reign supreme through it all.

The love and power of God holds up Mother Mary, and Jesus within this one vessel. Divine Mercy has been granted to Saint Julie Ann, through her love of God and Mother Mary. Their love is in the purest form and it is felt stronger every day.

## *MARY'S GUIDING LIGHT*

*The crowds surround him with love*
*They wait anxiously through the square*
*For a glimpse of his hand that waves so gracefully*
*Saint John Paul II, his light has always been the purest and brightest*
*Since the King of all nations own light guided God's lost lambs*
*Gunshot's blast, fast and furious, it unfolds at the speed of light*
*Mary's own guiding light saves a great man!*
*Scurrying and hurrying they flood the square*
*Searching and never aware that God and*
*Mary watched as it all came down*
*God's hand evident in it all as the love and light*
*of Mother Mary saved this great man!*
*Stepping into the light one more time to*
*help raise the spirits of them all*
*Mother Mary sent back to help rescue God's lost souls*
*To save a nation, a country and the world*
*Mary's guiding light is the same as God's*
*Shining and glimmering today*
*Love and light*
*God's own arms encircle the world*
*He graces the world one last time*
*To save His own heart from the same fate*
*Mary's guiding light shines bright through her new vessel of love!*

# THE SYCLE AND THE STAR

***Nightmares in the dark of the night and
God wakes me in a cold sweat...***

4:40 a.m.
February 10, 2018

Shaken from a dream in the night and my heart pounds out of my chest. It pains me as my heart beats beneath my chest. God shares with me as I wake from this dream; the importance of my journey and the importance of the deep lessons He shares with me, of the nightmares of His own.

Several dreams in the night and Jesus Christ tells me He will calm the raging bloodied waters with my own hands this time. Words of love, desperation and deep love for the children have been flowing to page after page and God teaches me; He sees everything. More importantly God feels the pain of every man, woman and child within the world.

Killing God's own life source. The choices that we make; on a daily basis are literally making Him breathless. Anger, fear, hate, greed, lust and then what we put into our bodies is taking His breathe away and the life force of His own soul!

Several dreams in the night and I will record them here.

I wake up to the word; **"Genocide"**.

I am reminded of indiscretions from so very long ago. Generations back and the lustful sins of our forefathers have created a large portion of this disease and the sick minds that are so prevalent within the world today. The 'devil' is present in too many of God's own children. Running around in fear and we forget to love one another as intended when we were created.

***Love and be-loved*".** God repeatedly has taught me, that is why He created human beings.

"The very reason He created Adam and Eve in the Garden of Eden. They were given choices to listen to His commandments and they both failed Him.

Eve wanted to prove her love to Adam. Adam trusted in Eve and accepted her gift. Something so simple and innocent has caused the world to spin slowly into despair.

Wanting more than what God intended for us to have and it wasn't supposed to be so hard. Wondering and figuring this picture all out. What happened along the way to get us where we are today?

The double-edged sword comes to mind with this whole lesson this morning.

Choices given was this double-edged sword. To listen to our hearts and to choose what's right or wrong. Too many of God's children have chosen again His love and light. Keeping the negative active within the world and God tells me I am so very naïve. I trust too much. I believe the good in others too much.

God tells me He adores that in me. A gift and a curse in the same breath. To love and trust like no other human being ever has. God tells me that is just one reason He chose me to love Him above all others. To write monumental books with Him.

*

Back to the dream of this morning.

*I am at a housekeeping job in this dream. Trying to clean up the mess of others is what I have done all my life. Trying to be helpful and work steady towards 'something' and forging on in the wilderness. Making a living and that is one of the meanings of this dream. I see me walking down the street and I am running late. I walk on my hands in this dream with a bucket in one hand and a white rag in the other.*

God tells me I am upside down of the cross with Him. The meaning with this is; I do not feel worthy to with the love He showers me daily with. I feel my sins and indiscretions keep me from being worthy of God's love.

*In this dream I see naked men and women. They are fornicating. Sins of the flesh and this has gone on for centuries. A lesson God has taught me is the 'fire in the soul". Desires and love, greed and lust. Things of this world and the aching of flesh for the touch and love of a real man. So many of God's children do not realize they search for "HIS" love. I have figured out my own heart and it was God who helped me come to understand and realize my own hunger was His hunger. To "love and beloved".*

Something that should be so simple, yet it is the hardest lesson of all. When we love and accept our own individuality we accept and love God. Loving our own temple and getting to know who we are and what we need to survive in life is a huge lesson to learn. It has taken me nearly fifty years to figure out the love I have searched for was the love of God.

\*

*As this dream goes on I see babies in this dream. They are laying on the ground and fornicating. They are literally eating one another. Sins of the flesh is the lesson with this. Child abuse and teaching the children of the world that it is o.k. to touch them and to abuse them at an early age. For too long this has gone on. God has seen it all. He has experienced every indiscretion with each one of us. He has taught me that He, sees, feels, smells, tastes, hears and knows all that we have experienced. "Not a sparrow falls to the ground without the knowledge of the Father".* Words from my own heart and they belong to Mother Mary.

God is so saddened by all that is going on in the world.

*I see in this dream a shop on the streets. I lost one of my own cleaning products out of my bucket as I walk on my hands in this dream. This bottle of cleaning products crashes through the window at this shop. It has foreign workers inside the building. I see people of all races in this building. All children of God. Lights and sparks of God.*

I am reminded of history with this next lesson. The sickle and star, is in representation of Jesus cutting the path for Mother Mary this time. Helping me on my journey with all that He needs me to know. However, the sickle and star has also been a lesson for me with Russia and the governmental upheaval. Trying times surround all of God's children today.

*As this dream goes on I see Jesus Christ; and God has brought this dream forward too many times in my lessons. I see Jesus standing and I see the burns on His face in my dreams this morning. I see Him scream as the chemicals that you cannot see in the air burn his flesh. The word "genocide" I believe goes with this scene in the dream. I have been warned of the "chemical warfare", several times over the past three and a half years. God sees and knows of all the evil with the world.*

Pain in my heart this morning as I wake up to the knowledge God sees more tragedy befalling on the children of the world. Warning's again this morning that He sees behind the scenes all over the world. God will continue to fall to His knees as His own children continue to run from Him and seek for things of this world.

I am reminded of the love story that I write for Him. God continues to ask me to hold onto hope. He reminds me he is cutting a path of righteousness for me. God is creating magic on paper through the dreams, meditations, visions and prophecy that He has shown me for over the past twelve years. Proof of God's power in love and proof to the children of the world that He is pure love and He hasn't left His most needed children in the world to the 'wolves' in charge.

Lesson with this*: Keep faith and hope alive. Open your hearts and don't run in fear. Trust in the Lord for He will shine a light bright down on* *all those in their darkest ours. God is not dead, and He will make His world great again; come hell or high-water.*

God reminds me this morning of His own soul. He tells me we are His own "Life force". We are eternally bound to Him throughout eternity. He has proven to me; that I have worked, worshiped and followed Him before. I have been faithful time and time again. I just forgot the love He holds for me. He is so very pleased that I am all that I am. A loving and supportive wife in His darkest hours of need. Trying to help my own husband and the children He has asked me to adopt as my own. The awakening, *"the dawning of a new era'* is upon us. May all our children be forewarned and forearmed with God's love and true light for we need a miracle to bring us out of this living hell we have created!

## ON HIS KNEES

***Jesus Christ prays before me and thanks me
for the love I shower Him with today***

12:23 p.m.
February 16, 2018

A painful heart this morning as Jesus Christ holds me up daily now. I feel the pains of all the tragedies around the world. Jesus falls to His knees before me this morning and thanks me for all my devotion to the Father throughout all space and time.

God continues to call me Mary. This morning I get more proof of His power and His deep love for me. Another manifestation and I am spotting. I have not had menses for over two years and this morning He shows me the love He holds for me and that I am His most precious Mother Mary. The woman who in this lifetime; through our love affair created the birth of the Savior, Jesus Christ over 2,000 years ago.

His power and love is immense! I feel it come through as I write these words as pain. More arrows that God and I share together as One in the

Holy Spirit. More prophecy has come true and it has taken me a few days to come to grips with the journey that God tells me I am worthy of. Writing books of love, light, faith and hope and it runs much deeper than that.

God shares with me I am the Second Coming of Christ. Through Him, with Him and in Him. The Holy Spirit has descended from the Heavens above and I am the Great I AM. The Father, Son and the Holy Spirit (Mother Mary).

A few months back I receive the message from God and I find Sanctuary in Jesus Christ's arms. I retreat to my bed to find out the reasons for my hidden anger and anxious heart. Mother Mary cries deep sadness and repeats: *"Dead Sparrows Falling Everywhere"*.

**News bulletin: Florida school shooting; another unspeakable tragedy leaves 17 dead!**

A gunman unleashed horror at his former high school in South Florida on Wednesday February 14, 2018.

(CNN)- Police say an Uber car dropped off N. C. at his former school around 2:19 p.m.

Wednesday. Within 10 minutes, authorities say he gunned down 17 people at Marjory Stoneman Douglas High School and left campus undetected in a crowd of students.

Now, as the 19-year old begins his journey through the criminal Justice System, a community is in mourning and investigators are looking for answers.

\*

Sadness creeps in, deep within me with this news bulletin. My own heart feels the sorrowful pains of the mother's, father's, sister's, brother's and children of all the victim's lives that were taken on this horrific day in history. Just another reason why God finds it necessary to take over my own lost soul in 2012.

Experience with so many issues. God knows I will not give up until someone steps forward and recognizes His books. His children are running with the 'devil'. Fear, anger and mental illness wrap up the true meaning with this news bulletin. So many lives have been affected for far too long and God is on His knees today begging for His children to open their hearts and let Him in to help lead them through these very trying times.

World War III threats being thrown around! It is already here. This is God's war! God's war on drugs, mental illness, healthcare crisis, child abuse, economic and environmental issues, let alone the political upheaval. It is time to stand in the light of God. It is time to bend down on your knees and accept His love.

A few months back I write the words; *"Dead sparrows falling everywhere"*. I was shown the vision of dead sparrows as far as the eye could see. I then here those eerie words spoken through my heart as I sob for nearly five minutes.

Visons of epic proportions have been shared with me for nearly three years. My first vision of Jesus Christ was over twelve years ago. As I wander the halls at our local mental facility. A calling from God then and He has taken over my entire existence. I accept the journey I walk on with the Father and the Son. I accept the arrows that God continually pierces my heart with. The visions of our dead children falling to the ground has not been easy to see. I understand God's own saddened heart.

God is asking for His children to love and be-loved! Yet, they continue to shut Him out and run in fear, anger and guilt. So much pain and so many tears fall around the world today because God's children continue to run with the devil. They continue to push Him out of every school, every public place, and the homes of too many of His most lost children around the world.

*Bella Louise Allen*

# *A PRAYER FOR PEACE*

*Mother and Father; we turn to you today*
*We open our hearts to let your love shine through*
*For our men, women and children*
*Who find themselves lost*
*We ask for your protection*
*For the innocent children who suffer greatly today*
*We pray for those; in times of unrest*
*We pray for those intrenched in war;*
*May you spare their souls undue pain*
*May you comfort all those in need of your love*
*We pray for the people of all nations may they come to together*
*In your name Jesus Christ and love one another*
*May you dear Lord; unite them as one in the love and*
*Peace of your Son, the Prince of Peace!*

*Mary Queen of Peace, pray for us!*

# THE WORD OF GOD IS THE TREE OF LIFE...

## *Verbum Dei Est Arbor Vitae*

6:04 p.m.
February 17, 2018

Behind on my writings and I am asked to walk back in time to last Sunday's church service. I attend mass at St. John's Catholic Church as often as I can. To receive the body of Christ has become something I crave. To have the eucharist in my body has never been as important to me as it is today. To feel the closeness with Jesus Christ that I feel as I sit in the Catholic Church is proof to me that this church is were God wants me to be.

I have always been a wanderer. I continually feel drawn to the Catholic Church. A love like I have never felt before. I find when I sit in the pew at Saint John's Catholic Church, I feel as if the angels that surround me will carry me to the heavens above. A feeling I could never fully explain.

God's kisses are felt strong as I sit in the pew. Conversations with Jesus Christ never stop as I listen to service. Hard to keep my attention on the message for the day, yet I am asked to share what I remember of this special service.

I get *"Saint Francis of Xavier's"* name this morning. A name that Jesus Christ has been bringing forward for the past few days. I am then given a slight nudge forward after and I am asked' *"I wonder if Saint Francis is here?"* Words from Jesus Christ this morning. He asks me to research this special servant of the Lord. This is what I found out about the man that stood in place of God and taught the faithful children of the world.

**Saint Francis of Xavier-** Born on April 7, 1506, in a castle near Sanguesa in Navarre (part of present-day Spain). With encouragement from his friend Ignatius of Loyola, Xavier devoted himself to religious service and became one of the founders of the Jesuit order.

The patron saint of missionaries and one of the founders of the Jesuit order, Saint Francis of Xavier sought religious converts throughout Asia during the 1500's.

Synopsis- Much of his life was spent tending to missions in areas such as India and Japan. He was 46 when he died on China's Shangchuan Island on December 3, 1552.

Early life- He was a member of a noble family, and his childhood was one of privilege-however, it was disrupted by his father's death, as well as by outside efforts to take control of Navarre.

**Forming the Jesuit Order**

In 1525, Xavier went to study at the University of Paris. There, he encountered Ignatius of Loyola, who had experienced a religious conversion while recovering from a war wound. Loyola did his utmost to convince Xavier to join him on the same path of devotion.

As I research this special Saint; God shares with me my own baptism. I was baptized and accepted into the Catholic Church when I was 14 years old. A young girl searching for peace in my heart and I found it within the walls of the Catholic Church. Jesus Christ reminds me He has watched me grow into a most beautiful woman over the years and I stole His heart.

I was baptized at Saint Francis of Xavier's Church in my home town. A church I found solace in while I lived a very troubled life as a child. A very rough road since then, and I have finally given myself fully to God. My life was 'overshadowed' by God in March of 2012. He reminds me today of my worthiness to walk as One with Him. Devotion and love is something He says is just one reason He chose me to walk this path with Him. Strong and willful and I never sat down my cross even though I ran and fell with it three times. He tells me I am just like Jesus Christ. Giving my all for the love of God and the children of the world!

Jesus Christ has asked me several times over the course of this journey; ***"Do you think you could walk across water"?*** I tell Him, "no".

His meaning with this question is, *"Do you think you will reach the Pope in Rome"?*

I hold onto hope; for if I don't God tells me it would crush His own heart. (a copy of "The Tree of Knowledge Mary's Sweet Vine- has been sent to the Vatican. Yet in my research I found out Pope Francis gets 10 mail sacks a week.)

God tells me as I sit in the pew at church this morning, ***"Mary, I lean on you every time".***

Father 'M' speaks words at service this morning, "Keep faith regardless of the costs".

God reminds me of the devotion I have kept even though the Catholic Church refuses to see His desperate attempts to get them to recognize the books we write together as coming from His own heart.

God asks me to tell Father 'M'; ***"Do your job"! "Open the books that Saint Julie Ann writes with me".***

\*

## HEARTS AFIRE

*The flames of love burn out of control*
*Engulfing my every thought*
*My every move*
*Our hearts afire today like before the beginning of time*
*My breath is painful*
*My knees are weary*
*My heart feels the arrows stronger today*
*More than ever before*
*Our children are so lost*

*Running in fear, hate and loneliness*
*I ask you all to pull together as one*
*Love one another*
*Support one another*
*The flame of love in your heart*
*Can be spread like wildfire*
*Compassion and kindness can help my own heart beat strong again*
*The flame of desire I feel for our children*
*is that of Mother Mary's today*
*Her love story is my love story for each of you*
*Mother Mary's journey is the same as your own*
*Our hearts desire is the flame afire within all of you...*

**I am asked to add February 6, 2018 communication here.**

I wake up from another sleepless night and God gives me the words ***"Iliad"***.

***"Iliad of Homer, Great works of Homer"***.

In the night I have a dream of Genevie and Sir Lance a-lot. God shares with me our love affair can compare to no other love story ever written.

***"The Mother of God and God; Himself bound together by destiny"***.

***"You were born with the strength of Our Son"***.

***"My love for you, is the greatest love of all"***.

Jesus Christ tells me; ***"This love affair can compare to no other"***.

***"God's love for me is the Greatest love of all"***.

*In the night I dream of Genevie. She has curly hair, long and flowing below her waist. Her face is gentle and very beautiful. I see her face over the shoulder of Sir Lance A-Lot. They are in a passionate union of love.*

Jesus wakes me with His hands upon my body. God is aroused in the night while I dream. We connect as one and I see God's eyes. We join as one in the ultimate union of love in the night.

He brings Mother Mary, Jesus Christ and Himself, in the heat of passion. We are joined as one today and throughout all space and time. We are the union of the Holy Spirit in flesh. Mother Mary, Jesus Christ and God!

**Bible lesson of the day: John 1:51**

"Verily, verily I say unto you, hereafter ye shall see heaven open and the angels of God ascending and descending upon the son of man".

# APOCALYPTIC PROPHET BRIDE OF CHRIST

*The wedding of the lamb has come; and His*
*bride has made herself ready...*
*And I heard a loud voice from the throne say," now the*
*dwelling of God is with men and He will live with them. They*
*will be His people and God; Himself will be with them and*
*be their God. He will wipe away every tear from their eyes.*
*There will be no more death or mourning or crying or pain*
*for the old order of things has passed away. These words are*
*trustworthy and true. Whoever is thirsty let him come, and*
*whoever wishes let him take the free gift of the water of life."*

8:25 p.m.
February 18, 2018

**Bible lesson of the day: Matthew 24:37-39**

**(37) But as the days of Noah were, so shall also the coming of the Son of man be. (38) For as in the days that were before the flood they were eating and drinking, marrying and giving in marriage, until the day that Noe entered into the ark, (39) and knew not until the flood came, and took them all away; so, shall also the coming of the Son of man be.**

I ready myself for an unveiling like no other. I hold onto hope as I am held up daily by the Father and Son of God. The Holy Spirit has taken over my entire existence and, in the night, I am taken to another world.

Jesus Christ touches me from the inside out and God comes forward with a vision and then I am lead down a path like no other human being I am aware of.

As God reaches out to me in the night and Jesus Christ joins us in union of the flesh I am shown a being from another time and another planet. I am first shown green and black scales. This being is huge in size. He looks me in the eyes as God makes love to me. I recognize that I am being taken to another world.

I see the dark circles of this being's eyes and there are slit's, like the yellow of a cat's eye. This slit is sideways in this vision. This being has long black nails (similar to that of a dog's toenails) as God makes love to me I am given the word *"Pleiadeans"*.

I research the word "Pleiadeans" and I find this information and the lesson runs deeper than dead and it connect me back to today; to the very reason God needs help from all His children!

## Pleiadeans- The "Son of God" and the Nephilim

The fallen angels that were cast out of heaven and the 200 angels that descended upon Mount Hermon, turned their eyes on the daughters of man and fell into sin. They come in unto us and they bore children called the Nephilim (Giants/Seed of the Serpent). The fallen angels mating with the daughters of men.

**The Nephilim-** Was cannibalistic, vicious and greatly feared for their size and strength. The Nephilim spread rapidly and both man and giant were full of corruption. The Nephilim were intended to wipe out the bloodline of God. God saw no other way but to cleanse the earth of this evil.

After the great flood, 200 angels descended upon Mount Hermon to teach man righteousness. The books of Enoch, The Angels, The Watchers, and Nephilim (with extensive commentary on the three books of Enoch the fallen angels instead fell into sin with the daughters of man after taking on the form of flesh. They gave birth to the seed of the serpent again, teaching man all sorts of forbidden arts. They produced Giants that inhabited and roamed the earth, the Nephilim occupied the Promised Land.

In the Old Testament they were called Anakin's, Raphaims, Zamzummim's. The many ancient Jewish sources tell us about the fall of the angels from heaven and the ones who fell coming upon the earth.

## It is written:

And I will put enmity between the and the woman, and between thy seed and her seed; it shall bruise thy head and thus shalt bruise his heal. Genesis 3:15

This was a prophecy of Gods bloodline triumphing over Satan's offspring. It fires signified David whom God chose to slay the remnants of the Nephilim in the natural (flesh) and it was Jesus who would alter conquer the spiritual Giants of sin (Spiritual) on the hill of Golgotha. This is also where the Philistine Goliaths skull was believed to be buried hundreds of years ago before by David (Golgotha means Hill of the skull of Goliath and possible Adam and or the shape of the skull on one side of the hill).

These Giants stood from 10-30 feet in height. Some Nephilim had six fingers and six toes. Some Nephilim had two rows of teeth on both the upper and lower jaw. Famous excavations and discoveries of Giants have been found all over the Middle East. Native Indian tribes wrote down the account of Red headed double arrowed Nephilim that were wild and cannibalistic. The tribe eventually stood up against them and set fire to a cave they inhabited. As a result, they died. Modern day authorities searched the cave finding accurate remains from the accounts of the Native Tribes. Many legends and myths that we have today are adoptions and variations of the original stories of the fallen angels on Mount Hermon. The Bible and another ancient Jewish source reveal to us that after death the Nephilim becomes just spirits, possibly the demonic spirits that inhabit the spiritual realm of earth today.

*

My heart feels the heaviness of Jesus Christ's own heart. God holds me strong and I fear not for He is a great God. All powerful and loving today, more than ever. Lessons today and I have opened my eyes and see the evil within the world of which He speaks. The 'devil' that runs with the lost souls of the world and they are becoming too numerous. Not thinking or feeling for anyone but themselves. God is searching for all the light workers of the world. From all four corners of the world. To stand tall and lead this world from their hearts. Stop running in fear and take a stand today! Defeat the evil within the world. Shine love bright and Be God's own light!

# EVOLUTION

*"I can calculate the motion of heavenly bodies, but not the madness of people" by Sir Isaac Newton*

8:00 p.m.
February 21, 2018

Laying with Jesus Christ and I am given another lesson that follows in line with God's previous vision and lesson of the day. Jesus gives me the word, *"Darwinism"*.

*"Our children are draining the life out of the Creator"*.

*"Gene mutation"*.

*"Too much, too much, too much"!*

*"So very cold"!*

I converse with Jesus as we lay together. Many messages of deep love and sorrow come through. I try desperately to love and support both the Father and the Son on this journey that God brought me back to life for. I am asked to research Darwinism for I have no clue what it's meaning is.

**Darwinism-** The theory of the evolution of species by natural selection advanced by Charles Darwin 1) theory of the origin and perpetuation of new species of animals and plants that offspring of a given organism vary, that natural selection favors the survival of some of these variations over others, that new species have arisen by these processes and widely

Bella Louise Allen

divergent groups of plants and animals have arisen the same ancestors—compare evolution.

**Evolution-** Descent with modification from preexisting species: cumulative inherited change in a population of organisms through time leading to the appearance of new forms: the process by which new species or populations of living things develop from preexisting forms through successible generations

\*Evolution is a process of continuous branching and diversification from common trunks. This pattern of irreversible separation gives life's history its basic directionality—Steve Jay Gould.

Also: the scientific theory explaining the appearance of new species and varieties through the action of various biological mechanisms (such as natural selection, genetic mutation or drift, and hybridization)

'Since 1950, developments in molecular biology have had a growing influence on the theory of evolution. —Nature

'In Darwinism evolution, the basic mechanism is genetic mutation, followed by selection of the organisms most likely to survive. Pamela Weintraub.

'The historical development of a biological group (such as a race or species): Phylogeny

'A process of change in a certain: unfolding

'Action or an instance of forming and giving something off: emission

'A process of continuous change from a lower, simpler, or worse to a higher, more complex, or better state: growth. A process of gradual and relatively peaceful social, political and economic advance.

'the process of working out for developing

'The extraction of a mathematical root

'A process in which the whole universe is a progression of interrelated phenomena

'One set of a prescribed movements

*"Survival of the fittest".*

A phrase God has shared with me before and it goes into this theory of Darwinism and theory of Evolution.

"Survival of the fittest" is a phrase originated from Darwinism evolutionary theory as a way of describing the mechanism of natural selection. The biological concept of fitness is defined as reproductive success".

**What is an example of survival of the fittest?**

"Natural selection, a concept first theorized by Charles Darwin, is the adjustments of genes throughout generations based on factors that help it survive. Sometimes this is survival of the fittest or the organisms that are better suited to the environment in other ways".

**How are natural selection and survival of the fittest different?**

"The theory of the natural selection is valid scientific theory, the theory of the survival of the fittest (Social Darwinism) is not... Charles Darwin's theory of evolution by natural selection is about the changes in species in response to ongoing changes in that species' environment."

**Why survival of the fittest is important?**

"Darwin's theory of evolution by natural selection is one of the most important concepts and organizing principles of modern biology... And because of its clarity, the phrase "survival of the fittest" is still widely used to explain natural selection to people interested in understanding the evolution of life on earth."

\*

Contemplating and wondering. Why are we all here? What is God's plans? Where are we all going when we die? There are so many questions, we as human beings think about.

As I am preparing to unveil my third book in a long series of lessons that God brings forward; I am taught so many things. None more important than the fact that God is *'absolutely breathless'*.

Jesus Christ shows me how broken His own heart is through all the lessons He brings forward. The negative energy within the world today is keeping God's own heart burdened and heavy. He has shown me "The Last Supper Table" has been set once more.

I have been shown so many horrible visions and it is with my own body that God allows me to feel what is happening in the real world.

Lessons in love with this theory of 'Darwinism'.

God has shown me the extinction process of His own children! Prophecy and the apocalypse are upon us. Things are changing within the lives of the children of the world. Sickness and genetic changes occurring at the speed of light.

God needs a revival of His own "Soul". God needs awareness of "love to be spread.

God needs His own children to step into the light of love. God needs his own truths of Science and Religion to be fully understood and accepted.

God has shown me the 'End' as is begins!!!

# GOD'S BRIGHTEST STARS RETURN

*Eternal Father, the Incarnation of Christ your Son was made known by the message of an angel, may the 'Yes' of Mary give us the grace to approach Jesus without fear, all the days of our lives.*
4:45 a.m.
February 24, 2018

Jesus Christ was God's truest light. Sent to give lessons of God's truth's. He spoke in parables and loved beyond compare to any other living soul. A miraculous conception and a story in history like no other.

God's own quest for Salvation and I am the new messiah. God's own messenger of love.

I am told repeatedly by God, *"You are my beacon of hope".*

*"You are my truest light today".*

*"You are the Second Coming of Christ".*

Mother Mary stands proud within me today. She feels my anxious heart and knows my fears. I am asked again today to take the veil from her face. To stand tall for the children of the world. Mother Mary prays long and hard for me to accept all that God has given me.

*"Believe in true love". "Believe in God's power". "Believe in the love God holds for our children".*

I do.

God has asked me on bended knee a thousand times to marry Him. I say "yes" again today. I will today, tomorrow and forever.

**Word of the day: Messiah**

**What is a Messiah?**

In Judaism and Christianity, the promised "anointed one" or Christ, the Savior. Christians believe that Jesus was the Messiah who delivered mankind from original sin. Jews believe that the Messiah has not yet come.

**What is the meaning of the name 'Messiah'?**

"Meanings and history of the name Messiah; Edit. From Hebrews word "Mashiach" which means "Anointed One." In the Hebrew Scriptures, Mashiach was used of priests and kings, as well as a future leader who would be both priest and king.

\*

# WAR AND PEACE

## *"God's war against Mankind"*

9:01 A.M.
February 25, 2018

Loving God to the fullest daily now and we converse every waking hour of the day. His love is felt so strong tonight and we love as a true husband and wife. Never a more romantic partner could I have chosen. Until death do us part.

We convers tonight and I see the love God holds for me. I feel it as pain through my own eyes. I first make love to God as we connect eyes and I hold a picture of Jesus Christ. Our hearts feel pain as we lay together. Those in the world, outside still run in fear and hate. He shows me the chaos on the outside world as I lay with Him. I see fighting, fires and tears too many. Blood shed continues around the world and God asks me to let Him take it from here.

I try with all my might and it is so hard to do. Visions throughout the day and night and the nightmares keep coming through. Somedays I do not know what to do with it all. He tells me repeatedly today, *"I am so sorry"*.

As we make love tonight God brings forward many visions. I first see my own heart. He shares with me *"You have always had a pure heart and soul"*. I see this pure heart and the vision is my own heart and it is white. Not red or blue. A heart of purity and God tells me I am still the purest soul He has ever created. A sinner today, like so many of His other children. Yet, God finds me worthy of this walk with Him.

*God shares with me a vision tonight of President Obama. He stands proud tonight and he has one hand in his pocket. He reminds me of a vision earlier in our communication; and He tells me of His love for Mr. Obama. A man who made history and he continues to make God proud through all he does.*

*I see the White House in my next vision and then I see a severed black horses head. I have had a connection with God before on this bloodied black horses head. It is in representation of President Trump. A movie in connection with this vision and it was the 'God Father'. The horses head in the bed was a warning to the head of the mafia!*

God tells me He will handle those who continue to spin the world out of control. He will take the world by storm with the books we write together.

God has been teaching me history lessons. Bible lessons and trying to keep my spirits elevated with songs of love and passion. Messages hidden within the lyrics for all lessons that He has been teaching me.

**History lesson of the day: Who is Saint Catherine of Sienna?**

Saint Catherine of Sienna- Italian Mystic

Alternative title: Catetrina Benincasa

Born: March 25, 1347 Siena, Italy

Died: April 29, 1380 (aged 33) Rome, Italy

Subjects of study: Mysticism

Role In: Avignon Papacy

Saint Catherine of Siena was canonized in 1461: feast day April 29 Dominican tertiary, mystic, and one of the patron saints of Italy. She was declared a doctor of the church in 1970 and a patron saint of Europe in 1999.

Catherine became a tertiary (a member of a monastic third order who takes simple vows and may remain outside a convent or monastery) of Dominican order 1363, joining the Sisters of Penitence of St. Dominic in Siena. She rapidly gained a wide reputation for her holiness and her sever asceticism. When the rebellious city of Florence was placed under an interdict by Pope Gregory XI 1376. Catherine determined to take public action for peace within the church and Italy and to encourage a Crusade against the Muslims. She went as an unofficial mediator to Italy Avignon with her confessor and biographer Raymond of Capua. Her mission failed, and she was virtually ignored by the Pope, but while at Avignon she promoted her plans for a Crusade.

It became clear to her that the return of Pope Gregory XI to Rome from Avignon—an idea that she did not initiate and had not strongly encouraged—was only the way to bring peace to Italy. Catherine left for Tuscany the day after Gregory set out for Rome 1376. At his request she went to Florence 1378 and was there during Ciompi Revolt in Junes. After a short final stay in Sienna, during which she completed The Dialogue (begun the previous year), she went to Rome in November, probably at the invitation of Pope Urban VI, whom she helped in reorganizing the church. From Rome she sent out letters and extortions to gain support for Urban; as one of her last efforts, she tried to win back Queen Joan I of Naples to obedience to Urban, who had excommunicated the Queen for supporting the antipope Clement VII.

Catherine's writings, all of which were dictated, include about 380 letters, 26 prayers, and the 4 treatises of II libra della divina dottrina, better known as The Dialogue illustrates her doctrine of the 'inner cell' of the knowledge of God and of self into which she withdrew. A complete edition of Catherine's works, together with her biography by Raymond, was published in Siena (1707-21).

\*

God shares with me tonight that I have written many books of love, light, faith and hope with Him. Not just today, but throughout history. God asks me today to continue to fill this most precious jar of hearts of His. The lives we have walked and talked and love together.

We make love in the night and God brings forward Moses, first. A man in history who wrote the Commandments for God. Tablets written and too many of God's commandments are not being kept.

*A vision many months ago and I see Moses standing at the top of the mountain with his tablets of stone. A huge wind comes up and he raises these tablets to the heavens above and the breath of God sweeps them from his hands and they come crashing down to the ground.*

This vision shows the deep anger God has for His children. Those who continue to keep his innocent children running in fear and making decisions that affect the lives of millions.

Tonight, Moses shows up and tells me again' "Do not lose faith". "Do not lost hope". "Continue to love beyond compare and God will prove the love for all the children of the world through your own love story". "Be courageous and forge on".

I receive strength from this message and I will hold tight to this vision.

As I make love to God I am shown a picture of myself. I am a child. Maybe around four or five years old. I see the Virgin of Guadeloupe and she stands in front of me. She fades in and out and I am amazed by the love I feel coming from her. I feel her gentleness and her deep love.

I am asked again tonight by Mother Mary to take the veil from my own face. I am asked to stand strong in the light of God for the children of the world I am asked to reveal all of God's love for the children of the world.

As God makes love to me He brings in Saint Catherine. Another special soul God loves very much. He makes love to Saint Catherine of Sienna through me. He teaches me lessons in His deep seeded love and this is another heart God asks me to place in my own jar of hearts. Souls of my past. Lives I have lived, and He tells me I have walked and worked with Him many times.

# THE CONCEPTION OF CHRIST

*"Her hands tremble and the love of God is
felt growing within her womb".*

5:11 a.m.
February 26, 2018

*"Blessed art thou among women and blessed is the fruit of thy womb".*

Prayers and invocations spoken to me from God and the whole spirit world. Never in my life have I felt so loved. Today has been another tearful time spent loving my Lord, God and Creator. He holds me tight today and we both find it hard to breathe. Our love has grown tenfold over the past few months and the ecstasy within our hearts is felt very strong today as another lesson comes full circle on the who and why God has chosen me to walk with Him.

\*

A few months back as God makes love to me He repeats, *"The seed is planted, the seed is planted, the seed is planted".*

An understanding with this phrase and the meaning behind me taking on the role of 'Mother of God' and the 'Mother of Mankind'.

Time is a continuum and God has shown that to me repeatedly. I feel His immense love as I write tonight. I feel the kisses of the angels within. The passion of Christ and I am all that I am.

As I come to understand God's true power He shares with me another body manifestation. Today I am experiencing sickness. He shares this feeling with me on and off. God and I talk about Mother Mary and her pregnancy. While she carried the Messiah within her womb. I asked God if Mother Mary ever experienced morning sickness while she carried Jesus within her womb.

So, today as God continues to call me Mary, He allows me to feel the morning sickness as if I am pregnant. I also feel my abdomen several times throughout the day and I feel the roundness of my belly. I feel today as if I am carrying the Messiah within my womb.

Lessons from God to help me understand the lessons of love He has for the Mother of God and for Jesus Christ. God shows me His immense love for me today through our deep connection of the heart.

I feel and experience bouts of tears. Coming to grips with the importance of the journey I walk as one with God. As, the Mother, Father and the Son of God. The angels and saints step forward so much today and shower me with messages of love and inspirations. I could never record them all for it is a constant connection with the Creator of the world. He allows all that has transpired, and I hold tight to my waist tonight and love God like no other woman ever has.

Bringing the Messiah to life through my own body. Bringing God's own Son to the earth planes once more.

**God's lesson today: "Through the love of Saint Julie Ann, the conception of Jesus Christ through the Holy Spirit was possible over 2,000 years ago.".**

God reminds me today; *"Believe it or leave it".*

I hold tight to Jesus Christ's hand and walk as one with the Mother, Father and the Son of God. I still believe all that the Creator of the world gives me. A love story like no other. We will make history together and God continues to ask me to believe in His own 'never ending' love story.

I do my Lord, today, tomorrow and throughout eternity!

# ANGELS WALK AMONG US

*The power of God surrounds me; and I see
and feel the angels holding me tight!*

6:02 p.m.
February 28, 2018

Opening heavens doors and God allows the angels to flood my senses from the moment I wake until my head hits the pillows. Never would I have expected so much love from the angels on high. The trumpets sound loud today on and off and I share the visions brought to me over the past few weeks. Revisiting some visions that I haven't recorded:

12/05/17- *As I lay in bed and just breathe I am brought a vision of an angel. She has the blondest of hair and she lays on her stomach. I see this angel clear as day and she is about the age of three. I see a single hand touch her shoulder and Jesus Christ turns her over. I see the bones of this angel and it is Little Miss Felicia. The angel that God placed in my lap on October 29, 2015. God asked me to walk and talk with Him while I wrapped my head around all that He wanted me to know.*

I cry tears long and hard and I ask God why He continues to torture me with these visions of this sweet angel.

He tells me; ***"Her case is closed".***

***"They will not find her body".***

***"She is gone to the heaven's above".***

***"Her father; out of ignorance, fear and greed took his own daughter's life".***

***"He was lost in the world that surrounds him and her life meant nothing to him".***

***"Drugs and money; and his next 'fix', his next high was his one true love'.***

215

*"He is lost in the world that too many of our children are drowning in".*

*"The drugs that continue to cause so much pain".*

*"So much death and it is just one more reason I have chosen you to help in a world living in such utter chaos".*

12/13/17- As I drive home from my overnight job Jesus talks to me. God shares with me; *"Please go home". "Let's rest today".*

As I drive the angels talk to me and I receive their love.

I feel her light kisses on my lips and God shows me her face and her tiny little lips and she kisses me just like my grandson. Miss Felicia tells me, "I will never forget your love meme". "God will never forget your love either".

*

12/16/17- I receive the word; *'cyclopes'.*

*"Saint Pedro Pio is present".*

I see the manifestations of Jesus Christ's wounds on my hands. I recognize Saint Pedro Pio is with me. My heart races and I heat up. I hear these words.

*"Your actions speak louder than words".*

*"Key tones".*

*"Key notes".*

*"Your life is a mirror image of Jesus Christ's walk with His cross."*

I receive the message from Pedro Pio to go to Father 'M' again. Saint Pedro Pio say; *"Tell him to do his job". "Tell him to open God's books".*

*

12/19/17- As God and I lay together tonight he wants me to make love to Saint Pedro Pio. I refuse Him this wish. I be Him "no". I go to sleep. I am restless throughout the night. God knows my heart and He knows I struggle with His desires to make love through the angels and Saints that make up who I am.

God and I converse in the early morning hours as I sleep. A dream in the night and it has hidden messages and meanings and God knows my love for Him will never fade or falter.

\*

12/20/17- As I connect fully to God and love Him during our time in the tub we discuss our contract. Our binding agreement from before the beginning of time.

\*

12/21/18- As I wake this morning I hear Michelangelo's name and I see a large blotch of yellow shiny paint. I am given the message from Michelangelo; *"You and God are creating a masterpiece for the children of the world". "Be patient and continue to love God as a true wife would".*

**Poem of the day:**     **The Master Weaver's Plan**

*My life is but a weaving*
*Between the Lord and me;*
*I may not choose the colors-*
*He knows what they should be*
*For He can view the pattern*
*Upon the upper side*
*While I can see it only*
*On this side.*

*Bella Louise Allen*

# GOD'S MESSSAGES OF HOPE

*'For hope is nourished in her' who is the 'Mother of Mankind'.*

8:55 p.m.
March 20, 2018

It's been awhile since my last entry into God's own books of The New Revelations. A hard road I have traveled since my full awakening to God's truth's. None as hard as the road He shows me lies ahead for the children of the world. Lost souls of God's own children are the very reason He has come home through me.

Scribes and prophets to help God spread His word and love to the children of the world. I, however try to prove God's greatest miracle of today. No counsel still from the Catholic Church. St. John Paul II asks; *"me to hold onto hope". "God's plans are great". "His love for you will prove to the world His power and strength". "You are His Beacon of Hope for the world today".*

Mother Teresa has stepped forward more times than I can count. She steps forward when the tears flow; and I am in despair. The visions I am shown daily break my own heart. The painful arrows of Mother Mary's are felt stronger every day. The further we walk as one, someday I find it very hard to breathe or go on.

God holds me tonight before I turn off the computer. I let the tears flow and try to come back to 'grace'. So much devastation around the world and it affects not just my own heart but the hearts of the angels within me. None so heart breaking as the angels that try to reach out to me for strength and guidance as they try to make it to the heavens above.

I cry tears for them all tonight. They love me for understanding the miracle that God has performed and the fact that I am God's own 'life force'.

I find the further I walk with Jesus Christ, it becomes harder to walk in the real world. God craves the love I hold for Him throughout the day. He shows me that somedays and it comes through as anger. Not anger towards me, but anger for my working so very hard to do all that I do for Him.

So many visions and lessons in His love and I can only remind Him of the deep love I hold for Him. I tell Him daily now, "no matter what happens or doesn't happen my love for you will continue to grow stronger daily".

We connect this morning in the wee hours of the morning and I am shown a colosseum. I am shown Daniel in the lion's den. God has tears in His eyes this morning and He tells me again; *"I am so very sorry for putting you through this"*. *"Your pure heart has done nothing more than love your entire life and I still test you through it all"*.

God brings in Adam this morning. He wants to make love to me, as Eve, through Adam. I feel our anxious hearts and the nervousness of two souls of the Fathers who have never been together before, I am shown God's own smile as I allow this vision and fantasy to go on as He makes love to me. He tells me; *"You honor Me each time you love me fully"*. *"Each time you allow My own passion to come through"*. *"When you love me as a true wife"*.

We converse today, and I feel we have come to an understanding to many things. None so important as the fact that our children need to know God's full truth's. They need to know how much God seeks His own children's love and acceptance. I see the pains in God's own eyes today and I cry long and hard for I wish I could help in some powerful way to wake our children up!

So many issues and so much devastation around the world. I wonder how in God's name, will His bringing me back to life and writing books of love, light, faith and hope turn any of this world's utter chaos into something beautiful?

# THE GARDEN OF EDEN

*"The snake in the Garden of Eden comes to me*
*in the wee hours of the morning". "Tempting me*
*and asking me to love Him like no other".*

3:33 a.m.
March 22, 2018

I sleep lightly in the night and many dreams come and go. God wakes me up, and my brain vibrates me awake again. Jesus Christ's hands never leave me. I feel them as I touch my own body. His love for me is so overpowering. We have come to an understanding this morning and this passion of Christ will never die. God's own deep seeded love for me, and He takes me back to the Garden of Eden.

In the night I see the snake and He surrounds me in the night as I sleep. God protects me from the evil within the world. My mind, body and spirit have fully merged with the Creator of the world.

God asks me to love Him this morning and I do as I am asked. Looking to please the Father; above all that I do.

I see the Tree of Life again this morning. God shows me-as Eve in the Garden of Eden. I walk naked this morning and God loves when I feel comfortable in my own skin. The first feminine side of God brought to life through the love of Adam.

The sun beats down on my delicate flesh. My auburn hair shines bright in the sunlight. I see Jesus in the distance. As He walks towards me I see Him change. He becomes Adam. The man in the Garden of Eden I sinned for. The man I lured in with my own love and desire.

Choices given to each of us. A gift and a curse since the beginning of time.

God's own plans and so many of God's children do not know the love God holds for them. The desire that God has, to reach out to each of them. To have a personal relationship with God is the lesson of the morning.

Keeping my heart open to the love of God has been my greatest gift from God. It has taken me many years to connect my heart around the deep lessons in love that God has been teaching me.

Love, desire, thirst and hunger are all deep lessons that Jesus Christ has taught me, as I walk as One with the Father and Son.

Sharing God's love. Sharing God's passion. Sharing God's own Truth's with the children of the world.

Photo By: Shutterstock

*Now the serpent was more crafty than any of the wild animals the LORD; God had made. He said to the woman, "did God really say, "You must not eat from any tree in the garden?" The woman said to the serpent, "We may eat fruit from the trees in the garden, but God did say, 'You must not eat fruit from that tree in the middle of the garden, and you must not touch it, or you will die," the serpent said to the woman. "For God knows that when you eat from it your eyes will be opened, and you will be like God, knowing good and evil." When the woman saw that the fruit of the tree was good for food and pleasing to the eye, and also desirable for gaining wisdom, she took some and ate it. She also gave some to her husband, who was with her, and he ate it. Then the eyes of both of them were opened, and they realized they were naked; so they sewed fig leaves together and made coverings for themselves. Then the man and his wife heard the sound of the LORD God as he was walking in the garden in the cool of the day, and they hid from the LORD God among the trees of the garden. But the LORD God called to the man, "Where are you?" He answered, "I heard you in the garden, and I was afraid because I was naked; so I hid." And he said, "Who told you; you were naked?" Have you eaten from the tree that I commanded you not to eat from?" The man said, "The woman you put here with me—she gave me some fruit from the tree, and I ate it." Then the LORD God said to the woman, "What is this you have done?" The woman said, "The serpent deceived me, and I ate." So, the LORD God said to the serpent, "Because you have done this, "Cursed are you above all livestock and all wild animals! You will crawl on your belly and you will eat dust all the days of your life. And I will put enmity between you and the woman, and between your offspring and hers' he will crush your head, and you will strike his heel". To the woman he said, "I will make your pains in childbearing very severe; with painful labor you will give birth to children. Your desire will be for your husband, and he will rule over you." To Adam he said, "Because you listened to your wife and ate fruit from the tree about which I commanded you, 'You must not eat from it,' "Cursed is the ground because of you through painful toil you will eat food from it all the days the of your life. It will produce thorns and thistles for you, and you will eat plants of the field. By the sweat of your brow you will eat your food until you return to the ground, since from it you were taken; for dust your are and to dust you will return." Adam named his wife Eve, because she would* become the mother of all living. **The LORD God made garments of skin for Adam and his wife and clothed them. And the LORD God said, "The man has now become like one of us, knowing good and evil. He must not be allowed to reach out his hand and take also from the tree of life and eat and live forever." So, the LORD God banished him from the Garden of Eden to work the ground from which he had taken. After he drove the man out, he placed on the east side of the Garden of Eden cherubim and a flaming sword flashing back and forth to guard the way to the tree of life.**

## EVE'S DESIRE

*Her love compares to no other woman*
*Feminine and lovely*
*My Eve from the Garden of Eden*
*Her own thirst, hunger and desire belongs to me*
*Original sin*
*Eve's desire and she belongs to Me*
*A fire burns bright in the night*
*God's own flame and desire is felt*
*Deep red and orange flames ignite*
*Her thirst and hunger will never be quenched*
*God's own desire is for the love of His precious Eve*
*The fruit of His vine hangs low*
*She plucks the forbidden fruit*
*And now she knows His love is never ending*
*Throughout eternity*
*He will love her*
*He will thirst for her touch*
*Eve's desire is God's own*
*Desire...*

# DANCING FLAMES

## *Jesus Christ waits for His bride at Saint Peter's Cathedral*

7:57 a.m.
March 22, 2018

The visions of love God shares with me will never end. Our love will continue throughout eternity. I see Jesus in the purest of white this morning and He wears a dress uniform. Living in the spirit world and my love affair with God, continues to be painful. Since Our hearts' flame is completely out of control. Dancing flames burn bright this morning, as God vibrates me awake. Bringing me to consciousness. Our mind, body and spirit have fully merged. We are One in The Holy Spirit!

I breathe in and out with God this morning, and He shows me my wedding gown again. In this intimate relationship with Jesus Christ and God, the Father, who Both love me so for all the love I have shown Them through the typewritten word and through the sacrifice of my life to them.

Today, I am opening another chapter of love, light faith and hope for the Father and Son. Our hearts are fully connected and burning bright today. We are predestined today. We are predestined to love like no others: The Father and Mother

As I love God like no other woman I feel His love grow within me. Over the course of this journey many lessons have come and gone. None as important as the deep love God holds for me through the Son.

\*

As I drive to Mass this morning I see Jesus lifting my wedding veil. He comes in close and gives me a most precious kiss. The wedding night has come and gone a few times. He reminds me of Our union as One. The Father, Son and the Mother of God.

It is a distracting morning at Mass. We struggle to stay awake. God holds me tight throughout service. He doesn't share one kiss now. He is tired. My desire to receive the Precious Blood of Christ is why we sit in the pew at Saint John's church.

I was given a choice this morning after our twelve- hour overnight shift. We could have come home and gone to bed or we could go to Mass. I needed to receive communion this morning. To continue to strive to be in His perfect likeness of God. Jesus loves me so for loving the Father.

The flames of desire within me have been fanned today. The energy I receive is straight from the Creator. His love for me will never die no matter where my feet take me.

## DANCING FLAMES

*These dancing flames within my heart*
*Bright orange and deep red flames of desire*
*The purest inferno out of control*
*These dancing flames of desire*
*Burn bright in the night*
*The rays of the sweet sunlight*
*Unite these flames in the daylight*
*Giving life one to the other*
*I breathe in and He breathes out*
*Igniting these flames*
*This dancing desire*
*The Mother and Father*
*The Dancing Flames of Desire!!*

*Bella Louise Allen*

# THE DIVINITY OF THE HOLY SPIRIT
# "GOD'S WHITE DOVE"

*"The Holy Spirit floats gracefully to the Earth one last time".*

March 22, 2018
3:53 p.m.

---

**Words of the day: Nemesis-** An opponent that cannot be defeated or overcome (2) Retributive justice in its execution or outcome. (3) An opponent or enemy that is very difficult to beat.

**Predecessor-** A person who held a job or office before the current holder. Synonyms: forerunner, precursor, antecedent (1) a thing that has been followed or replaced by another.

---

Interesting ideas as I research a few words God gave me two days ago. When God gave me the word nemesis, He then gave me Saint Diana's name (the Princess of Whales). At the first of his message God was comparing Saint Diana to myself. Then as I write the lesson I receive more information or thought impressions with His meaning. He leads me to the comparison between Mother Mary and then between Jesus and myself.

He then gives me the vision of Eve in the Garden of Eden.

I receive all these ideas from God. This is a huge process and God shares with me through this lesson how amazing He is. He shows me His thought process. How it leads from one simple word to many meanings behind it. I have been shown so many amazing things as I walk as one with the Father. The end of this lesson leads me back to the movie and documentaries that He has been showing me. All kinds of projects and lessons in love from the Creator of the world. Ideas far beyond me, His servant.

He wishes to bring history together for the future of His children. Through our own love story of Divine Mercy. These are teachings of

226

God own truths from the Father, Mother and the Son of God; through the hands of a once lost lamb.

God tells me the words nemesis and predecessor go together. This meaning behind Mother Mary, Saint Diana and Jesus Christ's own nemesis and predecessor. You can take it literally or metaphorically, I am taking the lesson as I was shown it.

The meaning behind my soul-purpose and the meaning behind my body being resurrected through God's own Divine Mercy.

Saint Julie Ann predestined to walk through the fires of hell, a hell I created on my own. Predestined to stand with the Father and Son. To stand in place of the 'Mother of God'.

To write words of love, light, faith and hope for the Father and Son.

*"A message to the children of the world:*

*"A blessed woman gave birth to the King of all nations. I was brought back to life to help bring Salvation to the world. To remind people about Salvation. Mother Mary stands strong with me tonight. We finish this book, for the children of the world. We bring strong messages of love, the love of God for the children of the world. God Created us. We belong to God.*

*"To all of God's children who do not believe in God's love for them: He is Pure Love. God is Pure Heart. His heart beats as one with mine, and no one can change my mind of this fact; ever"* ....

# "TRUST IN MARY'S INTERCESSION"

## *God's Never-Ending Love Story*

December 25, 2017

My Lord, God and Creator holds my hand tonight as we finish our own love story. Destiny and fate have brought us all to this point tonight. The birth of the Savior, Jesus Christ is the very reason for this special season. A promise given to the world so very long ago. His star fades tonight. His heartbeat slows as each day goes by. A faithful child and loving mother connects her heart fully around the love God holds for her. Mother Mary is brought back to life through God's own Divine Mercy, to write a series of books like no other. Prophecy from days gone by and the future of God's own heart source is on the line.

Mother Mary's heart cleanses and purifies an 'Angel of Mercy's' heart. Saint Julie Ann's heart beats strong after given the 'breath of life' straight from the Creator. Her life mirrors the life of the 'Blessed one'. A Pure heart through it all and her sins never outweigh the love she shines out to those she serves. Plans of God's since before the beginning of time. Resurrecting a love from the tombs. Blueprints of past lives shared, and Mother Mary takes over the life of God's own chosen wife. A love affair like never before. This story is a tale of two hearts merging as one.

Over the course of two years; sixteen books of prophecy written and truths from days gone by are brought to light. A devoted woman of deep faith writes God's own truth's. Saint Julie Ann reveals keys and mysteries written as parables in the Bible. The most famous book in history and God's own heart is on the line. Jesus Christ is back standing strong within the same vessel as this sweet Angel of Mercy's.

Jesus Christ's Sacred Heart beats beneath Mother Mary's heart and Saint Julie Ann proves her own love and faith in God. She stands strong and forges on in the wilderness. Sent back into the fires of hell to help bring Salvation to the lost souls of the world.

A time travel series written by the hands of Mother Mary, Jesus Christ and God; through the hands of God's own chosen bride; Saint Julie Ann.

Soon to follow; will be the additional loves story leading up to *"The Tree of Knowledge is Mary's Sweet Vine"*.

If you have enjoyed or found this true story inspiring or intriguing, please check out on Amazon.com or Authorhouse.com for first time author-Bella Louise Allen's; *"Miracles Among Chaos" and "Love Letters in the Sand"*.

You can look forward to the next book in the series *"Dancing Flames-Mother and Father United."* No release date has been set for this amazing book. This book leads you back in time as mysteries, keys and secrets of a love reunited is brought to life!

The books of love, light, faith and hope will continue. The books that Bella Louise Allen writes spans a course of twelve years. As Saint Julie Ann goes through the awakening process she wraps her heart and mind around the soul-purpose that God has brought her back to life to for fill. Jesus Christ teaches her God's own truths with Science and Religion.

This series of books gives new meaning to the "Di Vinci Code". These books in a series sets a precedence of understanding for the lay person, when reading and comprehending the Bible. History lessons, Bible verses, poetry, music and a deep love of God is felt throughout the entire series. Prophecy is revealed as the series comes to the publics eyes for the first time.

May you all have a blessed Christmas season. Always remember the love God has for each of you. God/Jesus Christ, Mother Mary and Saint

Julie Ann wish nothing but love to be spread throughout the entire world. May peace fill your hearts and may fear never over take your heart!

In Jesus Christ's name


Bella Louise Allen

# Bibliography

*33 Days to Morning Glory-A Do-It-Yourself Retreat in Preparation for Marian Consecration* Gaitley, Michael E. MIC:"2011": By Marian Fathers of the Immaculate Conception of the B.V.M.

*Jesus Who is He?*"1996": By LaHaye, Tim published by: Multnomah Books a part of the Questar publishing family

*Blessed Sister M. Faustina Kowalska Diary Divine Mercy in My Soul-* "1996": By Marians of the Immaculate Conception

*Peter and Paul-* "1944": By Morrill, Madge Haines published by: Pacific Press Publishing Association, Third edition, 1952
*The Scofield Reference Bible "The Holy Bible"-* "renewed,1937,1945": Oxford University Press New York, Inc.

*Beyond Suffering Bible-* "2016": By Tada, Joni Earekson by Tyndale House Publishers

*A Great Quote a Day Journal 365 Quotes to Inspire you each and every day of the year-* "2013": By World Traveler

*Love Everlasting Celebrating God's very special gift-* "1999": By Zonder Van Publishing House By International Bible Society

Prayers and Invocations from: U.S. C.C.B.- United States Council of Catholic Bishops

All Dictionary words from: Merriam Webster.com

# About the Author

Bella Louise Allen focuses her love on family, faith and the love of God. A loving mother of three and a grandmother of five beautiful angels. She resides in Bangor, Maine and has found a new love for writing.

Searching for peace in her heart and the love of Jesus Christ has led her to connect her heart fully to His. Finding happiness in her life finally and it was by the grace of God's own love for her.

A near death experience in March of 2012 opens new doors with first time author Bella Louise Allen. A modern day Catholic Mystic is brought love and light from the 'other side' and finds there is more to life than what the natural eye can see. Feeling drawn to the church most of her life and it brings her own heart to life as Jesus Christ holds her hand daily and she writes love story after love story with Him.

Experiential theories; brings to light many mysteries questioned by the church and many skeptics. Bella Louise Allen writes seventeen spiritually based books and they take the reader on a journey like no other. Traveling through time and space as she meditates and connects her heart to Jesus Christ. Prophecy revealed to a lonely child of God and she holds the keys to His heart. Jesus reveals secrets to Bella Louise Allen. She writes love letters to God's children. Those lost and looking for His own love to shine in their lives.

Providing love most of her life; to all that she has met led her to where she is today. Working in the healthcare field for over thirty years has given Bella the perfect chance to connect with people from all walks of life. Being loving and caring is nothing new to Bella.

Sharing with the world the love God has for His children is Bella's new passion. "Miracles among Chaos" and "Love Letters in the Sand" are the first two books in a series. Bella's own true-life story written as she finds herself. These two books help the readers see the progression of her own 'awakening' as she wraps her own heart fully around her soul-purpose and her passion for Christ; Himself.

# THE TREE OF KNOWLEDGE IS MARY'S SWEETVINE

In the 21st century, there are few books written as first hand accounts of the experience of complete abandonment to God. God has brought forward mystics in the past 2000 years of Christianity, individuals totally devoted to Him and the message of divine love and mercy. He has this message for us today. God's messages come with warning, warnings remind us that Heaven and Hell are real, that sin offends and wounds the heart of God.

Saint Julie Ann, as God calls her, has been a vessel of the Lord since she had her first vision of Jesus Christ in 2006. No words were exchanged. She walked down a hallway and knelt and kissed His feet. Then, she had a near-death experience in 2012. God returned her to life after surgery gone wrong. This was the beginning of her great adventure and passionate love affair with her Lord.

Like so many of the chosen ones of God, St. Julie Ann is honest and uncomplicated. She records her experiences in her own words, without theological training. She lives a consecrated life outside of a religious community and struggles to support herself and her children and grandchildren, working three jobs and sacrificing for her family as much of the world does today.

Although Bella Louise conveys St. Julie Ann's experiences from her daily lessons, visions, and experiences with Jesus Christ and His mother, Mary, the idea of Christ is with us and Mary within us is a basic belief of Christianity and Catholicism. You will be reminded that the words of love and devotion spoken by Jesus to Julie Ann are words He speaks to all of us. We all could live this great romance!

In a world without kindness, Julie Ann's teaching from Mother Mary, her words of compassion and care for "the children of the world," reminds us that we are always embraced by her maternal heart.

By writing this honest and true account, Bella Louise Allen provides you with a compelling portrait of what it means to live with total abandonment to God while struggling to live, at the same time, in the everyday world.

*Bella Louise Allen*

Printed in the United States
By Bookmasters